UTAH

KNOW YOUR STATE

ACTIVITY BOOK

THIS BOOK BELONGS TO:

_____

Manufactured in Versaille, Kentucky, in April, 2015, by Quad/Graphics

The activities suggested in this book may involve the use of sharp objects and hot surfaces. Parental guidance is recommended. The author and publisher disclaim all responsibility of injury resulting from the performance of any activities listed in this book. Readers assume all legal responsibility for their actions.

First Edition
19 18 17 16 15   5 4 3 2 1

Illustrations © 2015 Nate Padavick
All other images are from Gibbs Smith, Publisher archives or Shutterstock.com

Primary resource for material came from John S. McCormick, Utah Our Home, (Layton, Utah: Gibbs Smith Education, 2011).

Published by
Gibbs Smith
P.O. Box 667
Layton, Utah 84041

1.800.835.4993 orders
www.gibbs-smith.com

Designed by Nate Padavick
Edited by Michelle Branson
Printed and bound in the United States

Gibbs Smith books are printed on either recycled, 100% post-consumer waste, FSC-certified papers or on paper produced from sustainable PEFC-certified forest/controlled wood source. Learn more at www.pefc.org.

ISBN 13: 978-1-4236-4056-1

UTAH

KNOW YOUR STATE

ACTIVITY BOOK

Megan Hansen Moench

GIBBS SMITH

TO ENRICH AND INSPIRE HUMANKIND

Greetings, fellow Utahn! I'd like to welcome you as you begin your journey to learn more about the great state of Utah. We are so lucky to live in such a beautiful place where Mother Nature has been hard at work for years and years creating unbelievable landscapes! As an educator in Utah, I know just how fun it can be for kids to learn about our snow-capped purple mountains, red rock cliffs, dinosaur fossils, mountain men, Mormon pioneers, mysteries of ancient people, and so much more.

In this book, you will learn about the land, people, places, and science of our state while practicing core skills in reading, writing, math, science, social studies, and more. But, more importantly, you will have fun learning about the unique traits of our beautiful, wonderful, magnificent, incredible, great state of Utah!

Turn the page to begin your adventure!

CONTENTS

VOCABULARY

HOW TO USE A DICTIONARY OR GLOSSARY

When you want to know the meaning of a term in this book, you can look it up in a dictionary or in the book's Glossary (page 256). In both places, terms are listed in alphabetical order, beginning with terms that start with the letter A. Terms are easier to find in the Glossary because there are fewer terms than there are in a dictionary. Try it out!

Find the term GEOGRAPHY in the Glossary. On which page did you find it?

_____

Which terms were listed before and after GEOGRAPHY?

_____

_____

Find the term HISTORY in the Glossary. On which page did you find it?

_____

What does it mean?

_____

_____

_____

_____

What are the first and the last terms listed in the Glossary?

_____

_____

People use many different kinds of dictionaries, including dictionaries printed as books and dictionaries published online. Dictionaries provide a lot of information about a term, such as whether it is a noun, a verb, or another part of speech. Dictionaries also list multiple meanings of a word. Our Glossary only lists the meaning that specifically relates to our study of Utah.

generator
electricity

geography: t
people and pl

glacier: a b

Because they include so many terms, printed dictionaries have guidewords at the top of each page. These words tell you the first and last terms on the page so you know where you are in the alphabet. Online dictionaries do not use guidewords. Use a dictionary to look up the following terms:

Look up the term GEOGRAPHY. What information about the term did you find that was not in the Glossary?

_____

_____

_____

_____

_____

_____

_____

_____

Look up the term HISTORY. What information about the term did you find that was not in the Glossary?

_____

_____

_____

_____

_____

_____

_____

_____

Now you're ready to study the terms that are important to understand as you get to know your state—Utah!

UTAH'S PLACE IN THE WORLD

Each of these terms helps us find and describe Utah's place in the world. If you're not sure of the meaning of a term, you can find its definition in the Glossary (page 256). Follow the directions to complete each word frame.

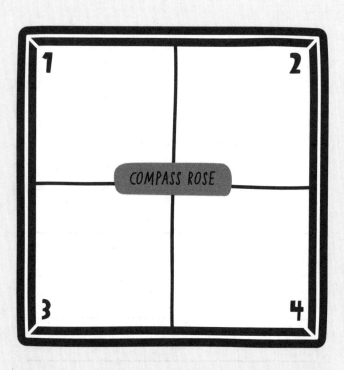

COMPASS ROSE

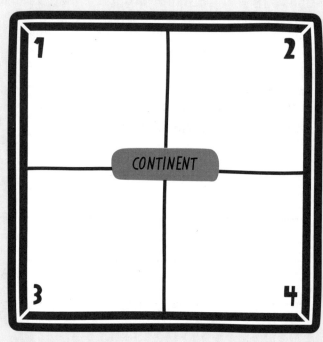

CONTINENT

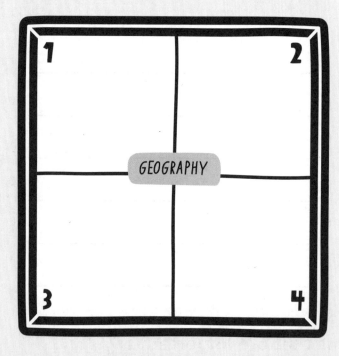

GEOGRAPHY

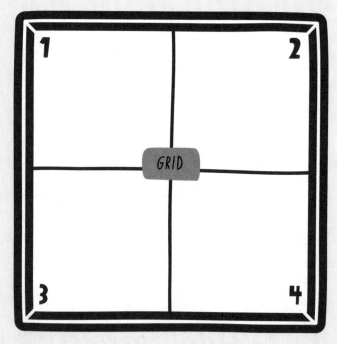

GRID

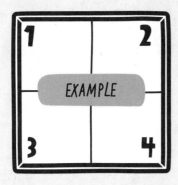

1 Draw a picture related to the term.

2 Write the definition of the term.

3 Write two or more words that describe the term.

4 Write any synonyms for the term.

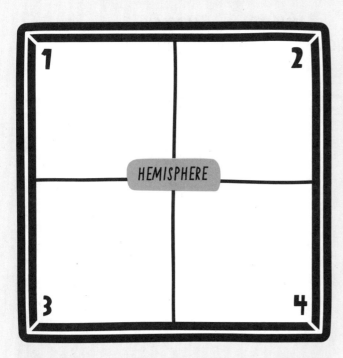

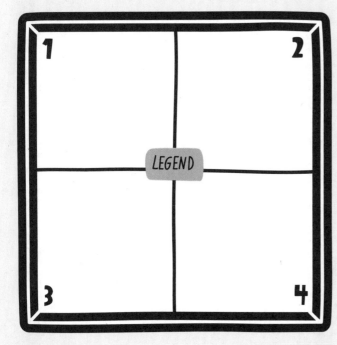

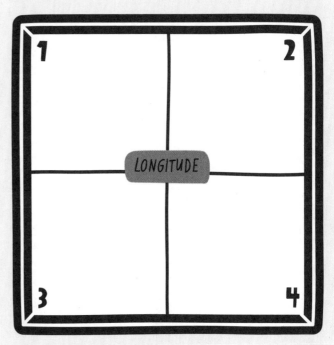

UTAH—A RICH AND RUGGED LAND

Use the frame to create a collage, a picture made of many smaller pictures. Draw a picture that represents each of these terms related to Utah's physical features. Label each picture with the term it represents. Use the Glossary (page 256) if you need help with the words.

BASIN	FOSSIL	FUEL	IRRIGATE	LANDFORM
NATURAL	RESOURCE	PHYSICAL	PLATEAU	RESERVOIR

OUR CLIMATE

The following terms are related to Utah's climate and the water cycle. Look up each term in a printed book dictionary. Complete the forms with information you learn about each term. Then use the Glossary (page 256) to help you with the definitions.

Entry Word	Page	Guide Words	Part of Speech
CLIMATE			

Definition as used in the Glossary

Sentence using the word as used in the Glossary

Entry Word	Page	Guide Words	Part of Speech
CONDENSE			

Definition as used in the Glossary

Sentence using the word as used in the Glossary

Entry Word	Page	Guide Words	Part of Speech
DESERT			

Definition as used in the Glossary

Sentence using the word as used in the Glossary

Entry Word	Page	Guide Words	Part of Speech
ELEVATION			

Definition as used in the Glossary

Sentence using the word as used in the Glossary

Entry Word	Page	Guide Words	Part of Speech
EVAPORATE			

Definition as used in the Glossary

Sentence using the word as used in the Glossary

Entry Word	Page	Guide Words	Part of Speech
PRECIPITATION			

Definition as used in the Glossary

Sentence using the word as used in the Glossary

Entry Word	Page	Guide Words	Part of Speech
TEMPERATURE			

Definition as used in the Glossary

Sentence using the word as used in the Glossary

DESCRIBING UTAH'S LAND

The terms on this page can all be used to describe some of Utah's physical features. Complete the table with information about the terms. You can use the Glossary (page 256), a dictionary, or the Internet to help you.

Term	Words to describe the term
ADAPT	
ENVIRONMENT	
GORGE	
REGION	
SEDIMENT	
WETLANDS	

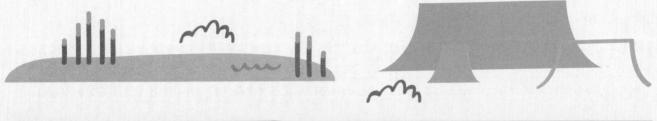

Examples

FORCES OF NATURE

Each of these terms relate to how Utah's land has changed over time due to forces of nature. Complete each word web with details that describe or relate to each term. And remember, you can use the Glossary (page 256), a dictionary, or the Internet to help you!

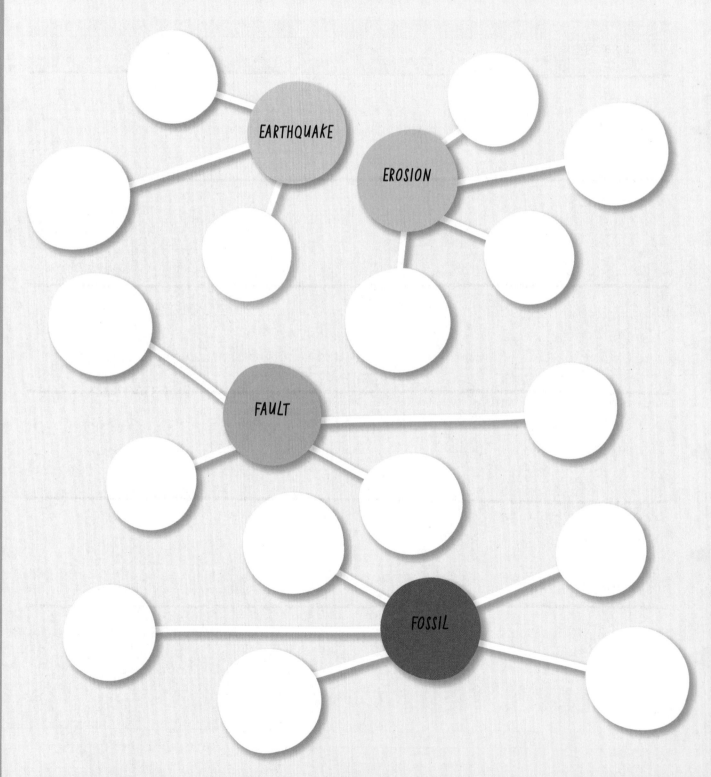

EARTHQUAKE

EROSION

FAULT

FOSSIL

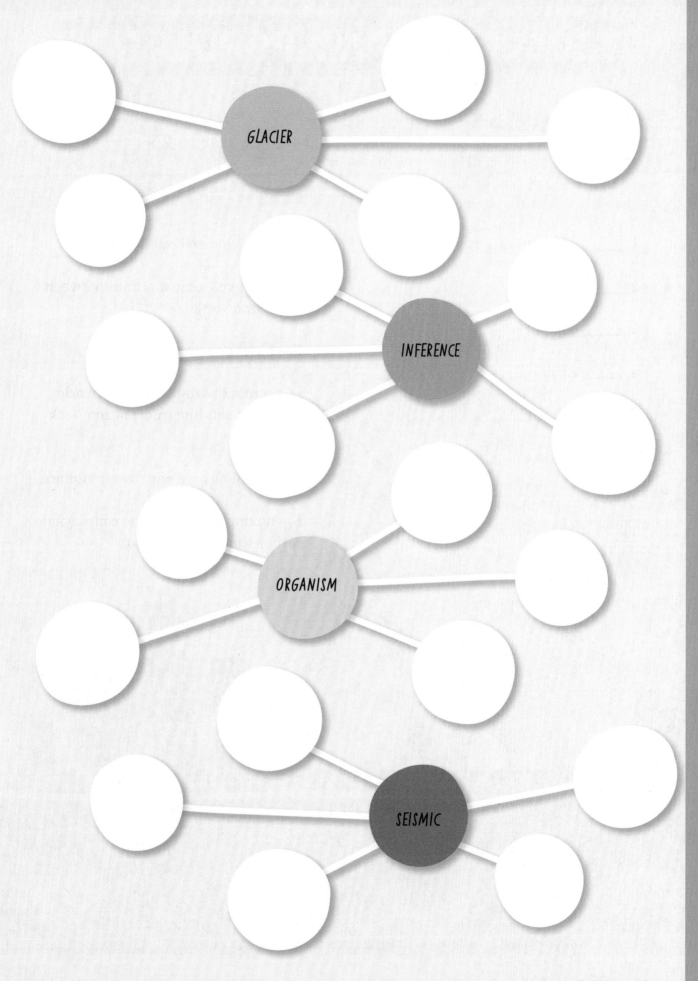

GLACIER

INFERENCE

ORGANISM

SEISMIC

GEOGRAPHY AND POPULATION

The terms in this activity relate to our three types of communities: rural, suburban, and urban. Use the Glossary (page 256) to help you match each term to its correct meaning. Then answer the questions that follow.

1. _____ communication

2. _____ commute

3. _____ population

4. _____ rural

5. _____ suburb

6. _____ urban

A – areas located outside the city

B – to travel some distance between home and work

C – having to do with a city

D – contact with the outside world; the act of sending information back and forth

E – all the people who live in a place

F – having to do with the countryside rather than a town or city

What is your favorite way to COMMUNICATE? Explain briefly.

_____

_____

_____

Has anyone in your family had to COMMUTE? Give an example.

_____

_____

_____

Have you heard of the U.S. Census? How does it relate to the POPULATION?

_____

_____

_____

Do you live in an URBAN area, a SUBURB, or a RURAL location? Give details to support your answer.

_____

_____

_____

_____

GEOGRAPHY AND INDUSTRY

Each term on this page relates to how people use Utah's land to create jobs. Use the Glossary (page 256) to look up the meaning of the first word on each line. Then write a sentence or two to describe how the two words are related.

1. AGRICULTURE, FARMING

_____

_____

2. FERTILE, SOIL

_____

_____

3. INDUSTRY, WORK

_____

_____

4. REFINERY, OIL

_____

_____

5. TOURISM, VISITORS

_____

_____

GEOGRAPHY AND OUR SAFETY

These terms are related to dangers that we can face because of our state's geography. Use the clues to help you unscramble the terms. Write the correct word on the line.

INVERSION   POLLUTED   PREVENTION   RARE   SEVERE   TORNADO   WILDFIRE

1. Not happening very often

AERR- _____

2. A mass of swirling winds that moves across the ground during a storm

NOTAROD- _____

3. A forest or brush fire that spreads quickly

LERIDIWF- _____

4. When a layer of warm air traps cold air and leads to a build-up of pollution

ERVINONIS- _____

5. The act of stopping something from happening

VTPEENNOIR- _____

6. Made dirty or toxic with harmful elements

UDTLOLEP- _____

7. Very great or intense

VEESRE- _____

Choose two of the terms and draw a picture in the box to show how they are related.

PEOPLE USE AND CHANGE THE LAND

The terms in this activity are related to how people use and change the land in Utah. Use the Glossary (page 256) to help you connect the terms to something in your life that relates to the term. An example is done for you.

Example: I can connect canal to __A STREAM BY MY GRANDPARENT'S PROPERTY__ because __A STREAM IS A WATERWAY.__

1. I can connect *CANAL* to _____

because _____

2. I can connect *ENDANGER* to _____

because _____

3. I can connect *GENERATOR* to _____

because _____

4. I can connect *HYDROELECTRICITY* to _____

because _____

5. I can connect *INTERACT* to _____

because _____

6. I can connect *TECHNOLOGY* to _____

because _____

7. I can connect *TRANSPORTATION* to _____

because _____

MANY POINTS OF VIEW

The terms on this page all relate to industries and topics in Utah that people have many different opinions about. People have different opinions on how people should be able to use land and natural resources in Utah. With the help of an adult, use an Internet search engine to find how these terms have been used in the news recently. Describe the situation in the news for each term.

1. BIOFUEL

_____

_____

_____

2. CONSERVE

_____

_____

_____

3. MASS TRANSIT

_____

_____

_____

4. POINT OF VIEW

_____

_____

5. SCARCE

_____

_____

6. TRUST LAND

_____

_____

THE GROWTH OF RECREATION

The terms on this page relate to recreation in Utah. Many people come from all around to enjoy all that Utah's beautiful land has to offer. Use the Glossary (page 256) to help you answer the questions.

What kinds of recreation do you enjoy in Utah?

_____

Have you been to any of Utah's many ski or other resorts? If so, which one? What did you do there?

_____

_____

_____

Think about your answers to questions one and two. How might people have developed the land for the resorts and recreation?

_____

_____

_____

What impact, good or bad, do you think recreation has on Utah's land? Do some recreational activities have more impact on the land than others?

_____

_____

_____

FIELD TRIP: HIT THE SKI SLOPE

A fun way to enjoy some recreation and get in a bit of exercise is to hit the slopes! Many of the ski resorts have year-round activities. So even if it is the summer, there might be fun things to do! Help your family plan a day trip to the nearest resort to where you live.

What is the name of the nearest ski resort to where you live?

_____

What season did you go to the slope—spring, summer, fall, or winter?

_____

What kind of recreation did you and your family do while there?

_____

_____

If you went at another time of year, what could you do for recreation?

_____

_____

What kind of tourist activities did you observe while you at the resort?

_____

_____

Did you notice any commerce taking place?

_____

What was it?

_____

_____

Do you think the tourist and business activities might be different at other times of the year?

_____

Why?

_____

_____

Pretend you met some tourists in your hometown and they wanted to know all about the nearest ski resort. What would you tell them?

_____

_____

THE STORY OF THE PAST

Historians, archaeologists, and scientists all have different ways of studying to learn about the past. However, they all study many of the same sources. The terms on this page relate to the terms they use to learn about the past. Use the Glossary (page 256) to help you decide which term best answers each question.

ARCHAEOLOGY   ARTIFACT   CULTURE   EXCAVATE
HISTORY   PRIMARY SOURCE   RUIN   SECONDARY SOURCE

1. Which term means the story of the past?

_____

2. What is the name of the study of history through artifacts, bones, and ruins?

_____

3. What do we call the remains of an old building?

_____

4. What is the way of life of a particular group of people called?

_____

5. What word is used to refer to an object people made or used and then left behind?

_____

6. Which term is used for a second-hand account created by someone who was not there at the time?

_____

7. What do archaeologists do in order to find something buried?

_____

8. What do we refer to as a first-hand account created by someone who was actually there at the time?

_____

LEARNING ABOUT THE PAST WORD SEARCH

Perfect your sleuthing skills and find the hidden words in the below puzzle. The words you are looking for can be found in the word bank on the preceding page.

```
W N I U R X E O A Y U J R G S Y V F C O
H G T O Q M T Q D R D J U L E R G I C P
Q Y B I T C A R R J T I Y D N R Q W U K
V L B D N G V F B U S I M R Y H R O F B
Y J I J N H A O T C N E F E R U T L U C
F Z D S R W C V O P A L W A O U U J S I
P B A Q I E X Q B M T Y E F C K R C K G
Y R C I O Q E S S C E S V B T H P Z O S
D G I E C T Z S O N R A W X R X V N Q S
I K O M S E C O N D A R Y S O U R C E Y
C I V L A Z G G Y J L A C V I T X P R U
G E X U O R W S E O E C N E I R S O D G
Z Y H M H E Y F F U K W M S V G T L M Z
Y F A W S U A S R W I Q M T C S F G D B
C R A D A T N H O R M J B G I I E R Q V
U N D U G T X Y C U K S B H U B A J O C
I Q G P D I G X U R R C X C W B P L T X
X P M J Y K S E G O A C F X P A I H J E
W V S Q C I O B F F K F E U O O O Q R O
S X X Y L K R D T E P S G J F T X F M S
```

PREHISTORIC PEOPLES

The terms on this page related to the earliest people who lived in Utah. As you learn about the terms, you might also find that they relate to people today. Use the Glossary (page 256) to define each term in your own words. Then describe why each term either does or does not relate to you today.

ADOBE - Definition: _____
Does this term relate to you today? Why or why not?

_____
_____
_____

CEREMONY - Definition: _____
Does this term relate to you today? Why or why not?

_____
_____
_____

HUNTER-GATHERER - Definition: _____
Does this term relate to you today? Why or why not?

_____
_____
_____

NATIVE - Definition: _____
Does this term relate to you today? Why or why not?

_____

_____

_____

PERMANENT - Definition: _____
Does this term relate to you today? Why or why not?

_____

_____

_____

PREHISTORIC - Definition: _____
Does this term relate to you today? Why or why not?

_____

_____

_____

HISTORIC INDIANS

These terms are related to the historic Indians who lived in Utah. They are historic because there are primary sources written by people about these Indian groups at the time they lived in Utah. Use the Glossary (page 256) to understand each term. Then choose one of the adjectives provided and write a descriptive sentence for each term.

Term	Possible Adjectives to Use
ANCESTOR	ANCIENT, OLD, SPECIAL, FAMOUS, POPULAR
CLAN	LARGE, SMALL, UNIQUE, HELPFUL
CUSTOM	UNIQUE, SPECIAL, TRADITIONAL, USUAL
HISTORIC	WRITTEN, SPECIAL, UNIQUE, OLD
HOGAN	SHORT, ROUND, SPECIAL, SMALL, PROTECTIVE
TIPI	TALL, TRIANGULAR, DECORATED, FRAMED, CONE-SHAPED
TRIBE	MAIN, SPECIAL, HISTORIC, HARD-WORKING
WICKIUP	RESTFUL, SHADED, ROUNDED, SMALL

Sentences

PRESERVING A WAY OF LIFE

These terms are related to the ways of life of the earliest peoples who lived in Utah. Look up the definition of each term using the Glossary (page 256). Then use each term in a question related to its meaning. An example is done for you. Try out your questions on a family member!

DESCENDANT   HARMONY   HERITAGE   LEGEND   PRESERVE   RESPECT   TRADITIONAL

Example: WHICH WORD STANDS FOR A PERSON WHO COMES FROM A PARTICULAR ANCESTOR?

Answer: DESCENDANT

Question 1: _____

Question 2: _____

Question 3: _____

Question 4: _____

Question 5: _____

Question 6: _____

Question 7: _____

ABOUT THE PAST CROSSWORD PUZZLE

Use the clues to solve the crossword puzzle. If you need some help, look at the terms in the word bank on the preceding page.

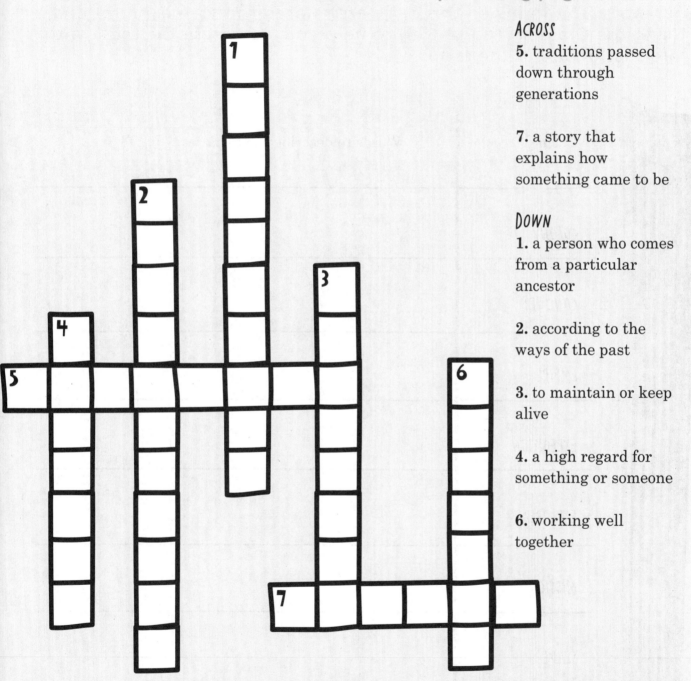

ACROSS

5. traditions passed down through generations

7. a story that explains how something came to be

DOWN

1. a person who comes from a particular ancestor

2. according to the ways of the past

3. to maintain or keep alive

4. a high regard for something or someone

6. working well together

SPANISH EXPLORERS

A few hundred years ago, Spanish explorers began coming into the land we now call Utah. They explored, made maps, and traded with the Indians. Spain claimed the land we call Utah and land around our state. The terms on this page are related to those explorations. Using the Glossary (page 256) to help you, complete the table with information about the terms.

Term	Words to describe the term
COLONY	
CONQUER	
EMPIRE	
EXPEDITION	
EXPLORER	
MISSION	
SLAVE	
TRANSLATOR	

Examples

THE FUR TRADE

After the Spanish, many other people began coming into the region we call Utah. Some came to explore, some to settle, and some to trap beaver that they traded for money or other goods. This period of time is called the fur trade, and the terms on this page are related to the trade. Use the Glossary (page 256) to learn the meaning of the terms. Then write a journal entry from the point of view of a fur trader using each of the terms.

BARTER   CACHE   FUR TRADE   RENDEZVOUS   TRADING POST

THE FUR TRADE MAZE

Being a fur trader was hard work. The trader had to gather furs and pelts from all over the place to make a living. Help this trader get to the trading post with his furs.

PASSING THROUGH THE GREAT BASIN

As time went on and the fur trade ended, more and more travelers began coming to Utah. These people were only passing by on their way to the west coast. The terms on this page relate to the people who traveled through the land we call Utah during this time. Imagine that you were one of the travelers passing through Utah. You entered this region for the first time long before settlers dotted the state. Describe your experience using all of the terms.

IMMIGRANT   PIONEER   WAGON TRAIN

_____

_____

_____

_____

_____

_____

_____

_____

_____

_____

_____

"THEIR FACES TOWARD ZION"

The next group of travelers to come to Utah was Mormon pioneers. This group of newcomers was different because they were here to stay. The terms on this page relate to the Mormon pioneer settlers. Use the context clues below to help you understand the terms. Then define the term in your own words. Check the Glossary (page 256) for assistance.

1. "New members were converts to the LDS (Latter-day Saints) Church."

CONVERT: _____

2. "Mormons chose Utah because it was isolated from other cities."

ISOLATE: _____

3. "By the time the railroad came to Utah, more than 80,000 people had migrated here."

MIGRATE: _____

4. "The church sent missionaries all over the world to teach people about their beliefs."

MISSIONARY: _____

5. "As a result, Mormons were treated badly, or persecuted."

PERSECUTE: _____

6. "They would be able to move faster in the beginning, over the flat plains."

PLAINS: _____

7. "At the time, many people in the East were talking about religion."

RELIGION: _____

FIELD TRIP: TEMPLE SQUARE

Temple Square is a 10-acre site owned by The Church of Jesus Christ of Latter-Day Saints in downtown Salt Lake City. The Salt Lake Temple is a monument of the faith of the Mormon pioneers. Besides the Temple, the Salt Lake Tabernacle, the Salt Lake Assembly Hall, the Seagull Monument, and two visitor centers are located there. Temple Square is also known for its beautiful gardens and wonderful holiday lights.

Talk to your family and plan a time when you can visit Temple Square. Write a few sentences about what you saw and a how it made you feel.

_____

_____

_____

_____

_____

_____

_____

_____

_____

The Salt Lake Temple is an amazing building. It was made using blocks of granite and it took about 40 years to build. Draw a picture of the Temple as it looked to you on the day you visited it.

SETTLEMENT AND NEW CULTURES

More and more Mormon settlers made their way to Utah. So did people of other faiths and cultures. As Utah became a growing region, there was a need for leaders and laws to help keep people safe. The terms on this page are related to the growth of the Utah and the need for leadership and laws. Use the terms and information in the word splashes to write questions you might have about the growing Utah region. Your questions should show your understanding of the meaning of the terms. See if someone in your family can help you find the answers to your questions!

SELF-SUFFICIENT
NEED NO OUTSIDE HELP

THEOCRACY
RELIGIOUS LEADERS RULE

Example: Did the pioneers create a democracy in Utah where the people rule their government?

1. _____

_____

2. _____

_____

3. _____

_____

LOYAL
CONSTANT SUPPORT

ENFORCE
TO MAKE SOMEONE OBEY
RULE OR LAW

4. _____

_____

5. _____

_____

6. _____

_____

FOUND
ESTABLISH

DEMOCRACY
PEOPLE RULE

LIFE IN THE UTAH TERRITORY

Soon there were enough people living in Utah for the United States government to make it a territory (not yet a state). The U.S. government wanted to have control over the laws and people in the territory, so they chose people to govern the Utah Territory. The terms on this page are related to that government. Match each term with its correct definition. Then use each term in a sentence that uses the correct definition of that term.

1. _____ legislature

2. _____ federal

3. _____ appoint

4. _____ territory

5. _____ representative

6. _____ petition

A – to assign a job or role to someone

B – relating to the central or national government of the United States

C – a group of people who make the laws

D – an official written request

E – a person elected to speak or act for a group of people

F – a land region owned and ruled by a country, a region that is not a state

CHANGES FOR AMERICAN INDIANS

The growth of Utah was not good news for everyone. The American Indians had already been in this region for a very long time. They did not want other people to come take control of the area. This was a time of much change for the Indians. Their land was taken from them, their way of life was disrupted, and many of them died. The terms on this page relate to this difficult time. Use the Glossary (page 256) to help you fill in the blanks. Then use at least four of the terms describing how you think American Indians might have felt during this time on the lines below.

1. *CONFLICT*: a serious _____ or _____

2. *DEFEND*: to resist an _____ made on something or someone

3. *REBEL*: to _____ authority or control, to _____ up against a

   _____ or ruler

4. *RESERVATION*: _____ set aside for American _____

5. *RESIST*: to withstand the action or _____ of something

6. *SURRENDER*: to _____ in to an _____

7. *TREATY*: a _____ _____ between two groups

_____

_____

_____

_____

_____

Along with the changes that more people bring, the Utah Territory faced other changes. Not long after Utah was made a territory, stagecoaches, the Pony Express, and the telegraph all made it faster and simpler for people and information to travel to the territory. The following terms are related to these changes in the Utah Territory. For each term, draw a picture that relates to the meaning.

FREIGHT

PASSENGER

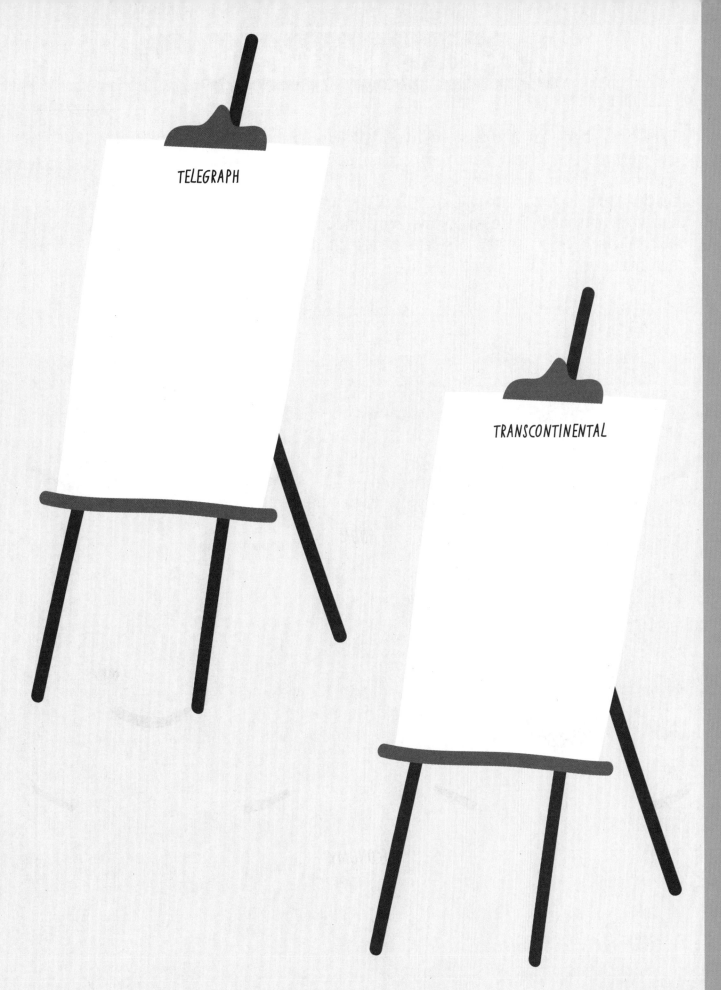

TELEGRAPH

TRANSCONTINENTAL

A CHANGING ECONOMY

The economy of a place relates to how people make and spend money. In the Utah Territory, the economy changed along with the people. The railroad helped new businesses grow. Things grown and made in Utah could now be delivered across the United States via the railroad. These terms relate to the changing economy in the Utah Territory. Create a T-shirt design that relates to the meaning of each term.

FRONT

BACK

BOOM

FRONT

BACK

ECONOMY

MANUFACTURE ORE

SMELTER

TEXTILE

FIELD TRIP: GOLDEN SPIKE NATIONAL HISTORIC SITE

The Golden Spike National Historic Site in Promontory celebrates the completion of the first transcontinental railroad in the United States. It is the place where the Central Pacific Railroad and the Union Pacific Railroad came together on May 10, 1869. Two of the last spikes driven to complete the railroad were gold.

The park is open all year long, but if you can plan a trip with your family to visit in the summer months, you can see working replicas of 1860s steam locomotives. Have an adult help you do some online research before you go. Be sure to take a camera and take photographs of the trains. Place of photo of yourself and a train below.

How do you think having a transcontinental railroad helped the economy of Utah? Explain.

_____

_____

_____

Do you think it caused any problems? _____

For whom? _____

Why? _____

NEW GROUPS OF IMMIGRANTS

The growth in the Utah Territory made people from all around the world want to come to work and live here. However, with fast growth and change come problems. Many of the newcomers were not treated well by their employers or other people in the territory. These terms relate to the changes that affected many people in the Utah Territory.

ACROSS

3. referring to a group with a common culture, usually a subgroup

4. a group of workers who get together to protect their rights and make their jobs easier

5. to separate by race

DOWN

1. treating someone unfairly because of the color of their skin, whether they are male or female, or whether they are rich or poor

2. to have an effect on someone or something

KEY TERMS

DISCRIMINATION
ETHNIC
INFLUENCE
LABOR UNION
SEGREGATE

STATEHOOD AT LAST!

It took almost 50 years for the U.S. government to grant statehood to the Utah Territory. With that change came a lot of planning for the new state government. These terms relate to that planning. Use the Glossary (page 256) or a dictionary to write the definition of each term in your own words. Then use a thesaurus, a book of words and their synonyms (thesauruses can also be found online), to look for suggestions of words related to each term. Choose the best suggestion and use it in a sentence in the final column. Not all the words in the English language can be found in a thesaurus.

TERM	DICTIONARY
COMPROMISE	
CONSTITUTION	
POLITICAL PARTY	
PRIVILEGE	
PROHIBIT	
STATEHOOD	
SUFFRAGE	

THESAURUS	SENTENCE

FIELD TRIP: PIONEER DAY PARADE

Pioneer Day, July 24, celebrates the arrival of the first group of Mormons coming into the Salt Lake Valley on July 24, 1847. It also celebrates other groups of pioneers who arrived before statehood and the Native Americans who lived here before the pioneers started settling in the territory.

The parade is filled with people and floats reenacting various pioneer groups pioneers and their lives. See if your family can plan to attend the parade and enjoy celebrating the day. What kind of floats did you see? Any covered wagons and horses?

_____

_____

What if you decided to enter a float in the parade next year? Using the space on these two pages, plan out what you want to do. What will the theme of your float be? How many people will ride with you? What kind of decorations will you need? Will your float have a name? Any other ideas? Write out the details below.

_____

_____

_____

_____

_____

_____

_____

_____

Draw a picture of your float, adding as many details as possible. Don't forget to color it!

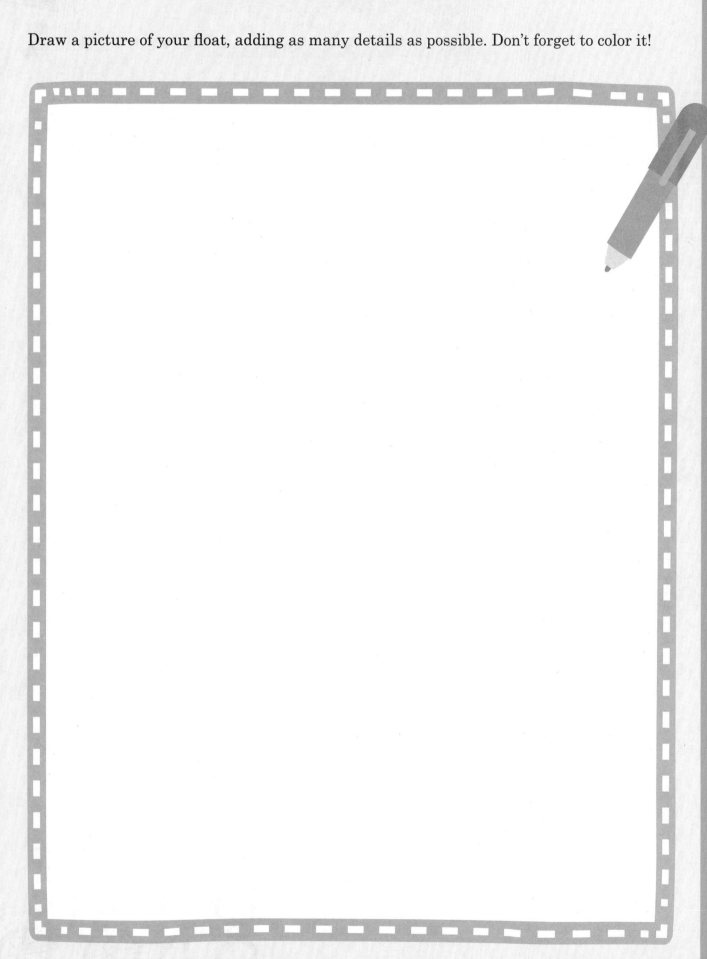

A NEW CENTURY

The terms on this page help describe some of the important issues in Utah as it entered into the 1900s. Look up the meaning of each term in the Glossary (page 256). Then, for each term, choose one other term and describe how they are related to one another.

1. CENSUS & _____

_____

_____

_____

4. PREJUDICE & _____

_____

_____

_____

2. CENTURY & _____

_____

_____

_____

5. VIOLENCE & _____

_____

_____

_____

3. POVERTY & _____

_____

_____

_____

6. VOLUNTEER & _____

_____

_____

_____

THE GREAT DEPRESSION

The Great Depression was a difficult time for many people, even affecting people in other countries. Many people in Utah lost their jobs and had no way to earn money to provide for their families. These terms relate to the Great Depression and the effect it had on people. Imagine that you were a journalist during the Depression. Write a news story to describe the situation in the picture. Use the terms in the word bank.

CHARITY   DEPRESSION   INCOME   MIGRANT   STOCK   UNEMPLOYMENT   WELFARE

TOWN NEWSPAPER
APRIL 11, 1932

_____

_____

_____

_____

_____

_____

_____

_____

_____

_____

WORLD WAR II

Interview an adult who lived during World War II. Ask him or her questions using the terms in the in the box to guide you. Write down your questions and the answers you receive.

ATOMIC   CONCENTRATION CAMP   HOLOCAUST   INTERNMENT CAMP
             LOYAL   RATION   SURVIVOR

FIELD TRIP: CENTRAL UTAH RELOCATION CENTER SITE

Did you know that there was a World War II internment camp in Utah? The Central Utah Relocation Center Site, sometimes referred to as the Topaz War Relocation Center, near Delta, was used to house Americans of Japanese descent during the war years. At the time, the U.S. government thought internment camps were the right thing to do. Now, people think very differently and see such things as civil rights violations.

Have an adult help you do some online research about the camp and find out about its history. There are still remains of the camp that you can visit and a museum with a lot of information. See if you and your family can make a trip to see this historical place. Can you even imagine what it must have been like for the kids who were forced to move away from their homes, schools, and friends to come live in a place they knew nothing about and that they couldn't leave?

Pretend you are a historian and you just found a diary written by one of these kids. What kind of things did he or she write about? Jot down some notes about how they felt, what they were thinking, and what they hoped for on the below lines.

_____

_____

_____

_____

_____

_____

_____

_____

CHANGES IN THE 20TH CENTURY
WORD SCRAMBLE

Unscramble the words and then write the letter from the numbered box in the matching numbered box below to find a very important word. Hint: if you need some clues for unscrambling the words, see the next two pages in the book.

NEMNADTEM

BOCTOYT

LVCII RTSIHG

GEARETSEGDE

VIRSEDE

JECIUTS

SOPGERSR

CHANGES IN THE 20TH CENTURY

During the 20th century, many groups or people began fighting to be treated as well as everyone else in our country. It was not an easy fight, and we still have more work to do, but some positive change began to happen during the 20th century. Below is a famous quote from Dr. Martin Luther King, Jr. Write how you think each of the terms relate to this quote and the Civil Rights Movement.

"I have a dream that one day this nation will rise up and live out the true meaning of its creed: . . . 'that all men are created equal.'"

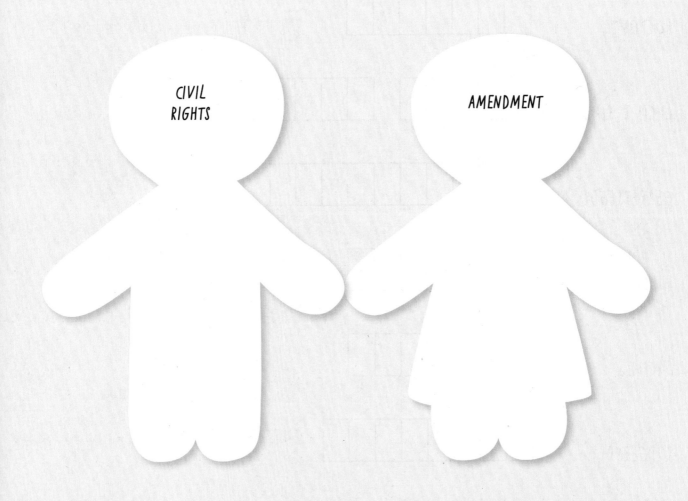

CIVIL RIGHTS

AMENDMENT

BOYCOTT

DESEGREGATE

DIVERSE

EQUALITY

JUSTICE

PROGRESS

ECONOMICS

To understand our state, we must understand the economics of Utah. These terms are important terms to understand in order to have a successful business. Using the Glossary (page 256), study the meaning of each term. Then, think of an idea for a business that you might like to run someday. Write about how each of these terms relate to your business idea.

My business idea: _____

_____

CONSUMER

_____
_____
_____
_____

DEMAND

_____
_____
_____
_____
_____
_____
_____
_____

ECONOMICS

_____

_____

_____

_____

_____

EXPORT

_____

_____

_____

_____

_____

_____

_____

_____

_____

ENTREPRENEUR

_____

_____

_____

GLOBALIZATION

_____

_____

_____

_____

OUR RIGHTS

Whether it's a country, state, county, or city, each region has its own government. And each government has its own laws and leaders. These laws tell us what our rights are and how we can make sure everyone has the same rights. Sometimes the most important government is the one closest to us. Interview a town or city council member to learn more about your local government. Use these terms to write questions that will help guide your interview. Write your questions and the answers here.

ELECT   GOVERNMENT   LIBERTY   REPRESENTATIVE DEMOCRACY   RIGHT   RULE OF LAW

_____

_____

_____

_____

_____

_____

_____

_____

_____

_____

_____

WHO WE ARE TODAY

Today our state is very diverse with large Hispanic, Latino, and refugee populations. Fill in each web with details about these cultures and groups of people. With the help of an adult, you can use the Internet to find a lot of great information about these and other groups of people in Utah.

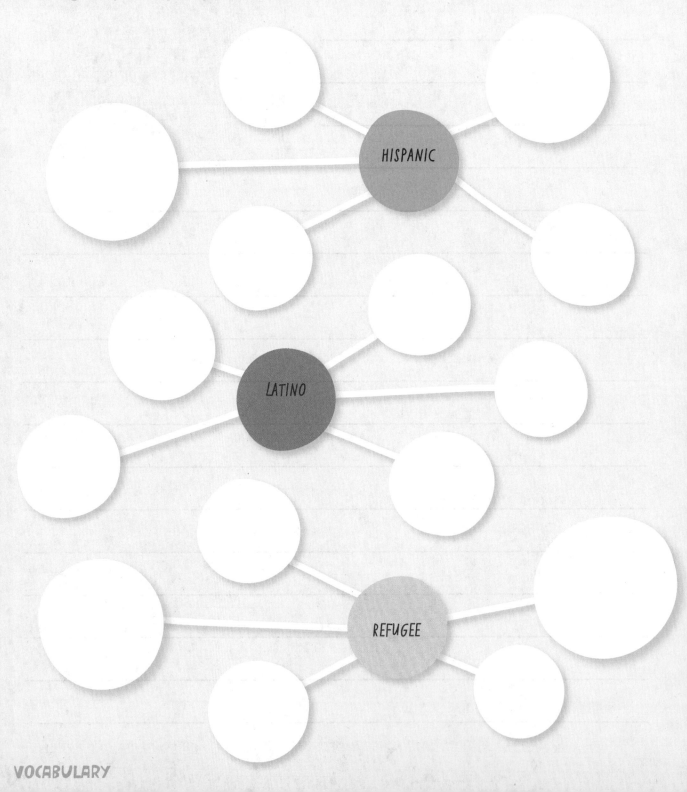

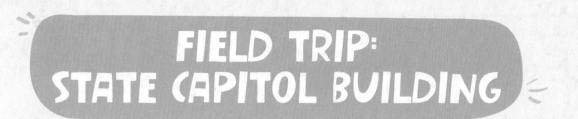

FIELD TRIP: STATE CAPITOL BUILDING

The Utah State Capitol Building in Salt Lake City is the house of the government for the state of Utah. You can take a guided tour of the building by calling ahead and scheduling a day and time for your visit. Or, you can just stop by and visit on your own.

Have an adult help you do some online research before you visit. Make a list of things you would like to see. When you get to the capitol, go on a scavenger hunt to find the items on your list. Be sure to check them off when you find them.

☐ _____
☐ _____
☐ _____
☐ _____
☐ _____
☐ _____
☐ _____
☐ _____
☐ _____
☐ _____
☐ _____
☐ _____
☐ _____
☐ _____

OUR RESPONSIBILITIES

Our governments guarantee us certain rights. However, along with those rights, we have responsibilities that we need to perform, such as voting, paying taxes, and helping people in our community. These terms all relate to our responsibilities as citizens of the United States. For each term, write ideas related to the term that you can do to be a responsible citizen.

ALLEGIANCE

_____

_____

_____

CITIZEN

_____

_____

_____

CIVIC ORGANIZATION

_____

_____

_____

GUARANTEE

RESPONSIBILITY

TAX

VOLUNTEER

GEOGRAPHY & SOCIAL STUDIES

MY PLACE IN THE WORLD

Before we can understand our state, we need to understand where our state fits in and where we fit in! Complete the diagram below starting with yourself to help you understand exactly where you are in the world!

I
am a
part of a
family,

Which is part of

_____
(neighborhood)

Which is part of

_____
(city/town)

Which is part of

_____
(county)

Which is part of

_____
(state)

Which is part of the

_____
(region)

Which is part of

_____
(country)

Which is part of

_____
(continent)

Which is part of

_____
(hemisphere)

Which is part of the planet Earth!

HEMISPHERES

N

W   E

S

To help us understand where things are located, we pretend the Earth is cut into two equal pieces. Each half is called a hemisphere.

Hemi means half. Sphere means a round, solid shape
Put them together: Half of a round, solid shape

The equator divides the Earth into hemispheres. The area north of the equator to the north pole is the northern hemisphere. The area south of the equator to the south pole is the southern hemisphere. Because Utah is north of the equator, it is in the northern hemisphere.

The prime meridian splits the Earth in half a different way. The area west of the prime meridian is the western hemisphere. The area east of the prime meridian is the eastern hemisphere. Utah is in the western hemisphere.

Use the compass to help you determine which hemisphere is which. Label each hemisphere.

| NORTHERN HEMISPHERE | SOUTHERN HEMISPHERE | WESTERN HEMISPHERE |

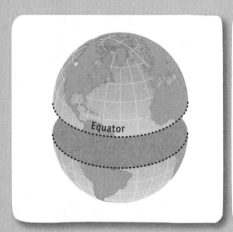

MY HOME GEOGRAPHY

Geography is the study of the land, water, plants, animals, and people of a place. What is the geography like where you live? Use this chart to help you study and learn more about the geography where you live! Share your findings with a family member.

What **landforms** do you see around your house? (mountains, valleys, basins, plateaus)

What sources of **water** are near your home? (lakes, rivers, streams)

What **plant life** is common where you live?

What **animals** live near where you live?

Describe the **people** near where you live. (age, family makeup, religion, jobs)

NEIGHBORHOOD WALK

Take a walk around your neighborhood, the exact same path, at three different times on the same day—in the morning, at midday, and in the evening. What do you observe? Make a list for each walk noting what you see. People, animals, plants, cars, weather, bugs— who knows what else there may be?!

1. MORNING

_____

2. MIDDAY

_____

3. EVENING

_____

Did everything look the same all day long? Or did you observe something different depending on the time of day? Write your observations below.

_____

_____

_____

What day of the week was it when you went on your walk? Do you think you might see something different on other days?

_____

_____

_____

BUILD A COMPASS

Over 1,000 years ago, the Chinese discovered that a swinging magnet always pointed north. This swinging magnet became the first compass. During the 1400s, Europeans improved the compass. Sailors, who were miles away from shore, used it to figure out direction. Today, many people use a GPS to find directions and locate places. You can make a compass at home!

YOU WILL NEED:

A plastic lid or shallow bowl
A needle or straight pin
A bar magnet
A slice of cork, Styrofoam, or
    the top of a plastic milk jug
Some water

INSTRUCTIONS:

1. Have an adult help you slice off a piece of cork.
2. Magnetize your needle! Hold the needle in one hand and the bar magnet in the other.
3. Taking care to only move in one direction, not back and forth, slide one end of the bar magnet along the length of the needle. Lift up the magnet and slide in the same direction again. Repeat this at least 50 times.
4. Pour some water in the plastic lid.
5. Place the cork in the water and make sure there is enough water for the cork to float.
6. Lay the needle on top of the cork. Make sure the needle is balanced well.
7. The needle will move until it points north. This may take a moment.
8. If your needle isn't pointing north, repeat step two.

CONGRATULATIONS! YOU HAVE MADE A COMPASS!

MAP TERMS WORD SEARCH

It is important to be familiar with terms associated with maps. The terms help you understand the information the maps are providing. Using the terms in the word box, circle the hidden words in the puzzle.

COMPASS ROSE   EAST   EQUATOR   HEMISPHERE   LEGEND   NORTH
PRIME MERIDIAN   SCALE OF MILES   SOUTH   WEST

```
J Z Q U P B D S C A L E O F M I L E S H
P U N W S R B E P H E Q Z J N D Z V E B
L E G E N D I D O O P K N B I Q M M C M
Q K V F E Y Y M W N L I K Z X S I F X J
T W T O H M N M E U D J W F N S M C Z X
E Q U A T O R H C M H L R Z P M N X G Y
K H A F L K Q X X L E N Q H T W G M G K
W F U B K I G M X U K R E T T F R O E O
E Q J Z F V G R D J R I V M S D E J M
U U C O R R V H Z T E Y I D B G A R S J
Z U A V N H X E E T S O O G I V T E U H
O D C L Z E F P M H J Z W O L A D P F I
J J T P D S Y I E H R I C V Z M N K Y W
J H S R G F Q D C G F R Z D B U W F A R
N H H U W J Q T X S P I F Z O G L P S X
O T T C Y E F J S H E C F G B D E E U R
R S U U C J I Q G C O M P A S S R O S E
T E Y T O K A O I N O V F Y A G R R Z F
H W L W C S X P W W U Q V W D P F F V Q
B B L U U M P B A W N O Z X W D T Q V Z
```

A MAP BY ANY OTHER NAME . . . WOULD STILL BE A MAP

Maps are like pictures. They say a lot with a few words. Maps are important tools of geography, and they have many purposes.

Although maps may show different information, they usually have some common features: a title, a compass rose, a scale of miles, a legend (or key) to explain what symbols mean, and a grid. Study this map of Utah to answer the questions.

MINING CITIES IN UTAH

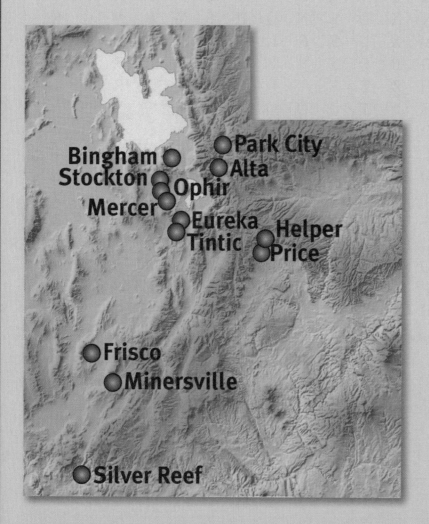

What do you notice about the location of the mining cities in Utah?

_____

_____

_____

_____

_____

_____

Finish this sentence to make a generalization about mining in Utah: Most of the mining cities in Utah are located

_____

_____

_____

_____

_____

_____

GEOGRAPHY & SOCIAL STUDIES

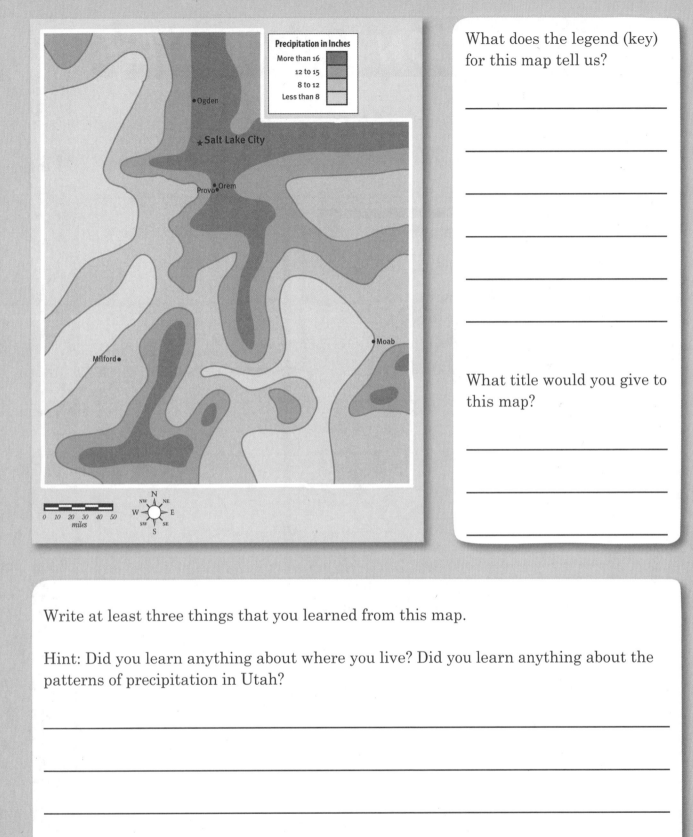

Precipitation in Inches

More than 16
12 to 15
8 to 12
Less than 8

•Ogden

★Salt Lake City

Provo• •Orem

Milford•

•Moab

N
NW NE
W   E
SW SE
S

0 10 20 30 40 50
miles

What does the legend (key) for this map tell us?

_____

_____

_____

_____

_____

_____

What title would you give to this map?

_____

_____

_____

Write at least three things that you learned from this map.

Hint: Did you learn anything about where you live? Did you learn anything about the patterns of precipitation in Utah?

_____

_____

_____

_____

_____

This map shows the population of Utah's towns and cities. Study the map and answer the questions.

Population: Cities and Towns, 2008

▨	0 - 1,000
▨	1,001 - 5,000
▨	5,001 - 20,000
▨	**20,0001 - 50,000**
▨	**More than 50,000**

1. Which color represents areas with the highest populations

_____

2. Which color represents areas with the smallest populations?

_____

3. What generalization can you make about Utah's cities with the highest populations?

_____

_____

_____

_____

_____

_____

4. What are three cities with some of the smallest populations?

_____

_____

_____

5. What are three cities with some of the largest populations?

_____

_____

_____

6. According to the map, what is the population where you live?

_____

7. If you were given a piece of land in western Utah, near Wendover, to start a community, what challenges might keep your community from growing?

_____

_____

_____

_____

_____

_____

_____

_____

LAND FEATURES

Read about the land features found in Utah. Then label each of the land features on the map.

Mountains are high landforms with large bases and small peaks. A long line of mountains is called a **mountain range**. When snow in the mountains melts, it fills **rivers** and **lakes**. **Rivers** and **streams** run down to the valleys. This provides water for people and farms. **Valleys** are smaller basins found between mountain ranges. Most cities, farms, and ranches are in basins and valleys.

Basins are large, low, flat areas surrounded by mountains or high plateaus. They are shaped like huge bowls. About half of Utah is part of a large basin that stretches across several states. It is called the Great Basin. **Plateaus** are high, wide, flat areas of land. They often end with steep cliffs or **mountains**. From above, they look like tables or wide steps many miles across. Over time, wind and water cut deep canyons and shapes into **plateaus**.

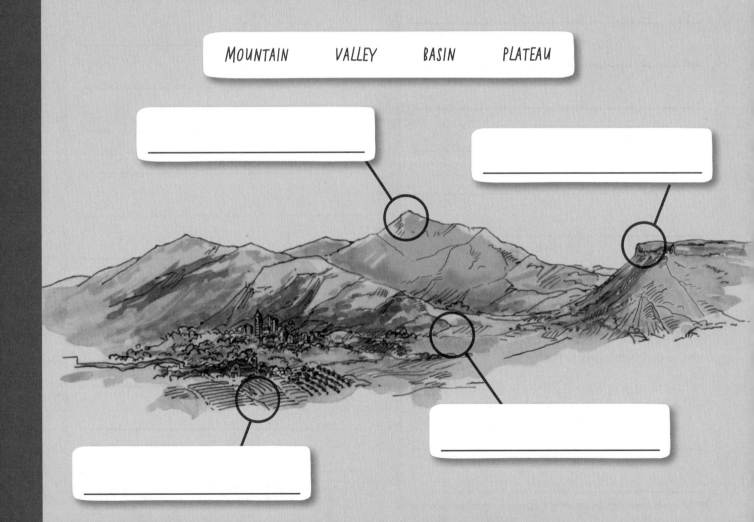

MOUNTAIN   VALLEY   BASIN   PLATEAU

LAND FEATURES CROSSWORD PUZZLE

Using the clues, solve the puzzle. If you need a hint, see the terms on the Land Features page next to this page.

ACROSS
2. run down to the valleys

6. provides water for people and farms

7. landforms with large bases and small peaks

DOWN
1. smaller basins found between mountain ranges

3. high, wide, flat areas of land

4. large, low flat areas surrounded by mountains

5. melted snow fills

7. a long line of mountains

PICTURING UTAH'S LAND REGIONS

There are three land regions in Utah. Each region is defined by its common landforms. Even though each region is made up of one main type of land, it may still contain small amounts of other types.

Utah's Land Regions

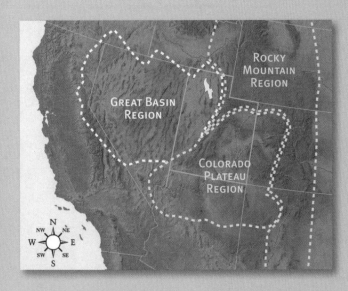

Draw a picture of a scene from Utah's Colorado Plateau Region.

The Colorado Plateau Region

In southeastern Utah the land becomes high, flat, and rocky. This is the Colorado Plateau region, the largest land region in Utah. In this region colorful cliffs can rise a thousand feet above the valley floor and stretch for hundreds of miles. Over millions of years, wind and rain have carved many different and amazing rock formations. The Colorado and Green Rivers have cut deep canyons and gorges through the region. This region gets very little rain. All five of Utah's national parks are in this region: Arches, Bryce Canyon, Canyonlands, Capitol Reef, and Zion.

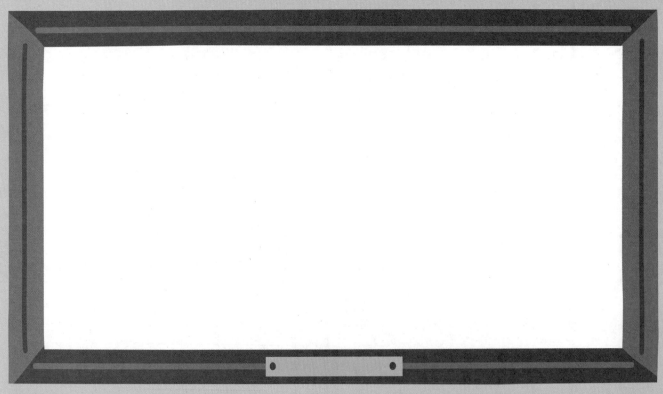

GEOGRAPHY & SOCIAL STUDIES

The Great Basin Region

In this region most of the land is flat with a hot and dry climate. It is one of the driest deserts in the United States. However, the Great Basin is considered a cold desert because in the winter it can get below freezing and snow is common. Most of the people in Utah live in this region. Our biggest cities and towns are here with Salt Lake City as the largest city.

Draw a picture of a scene from Utah's Great Basin Region.

The Rocky Mountain Region

Our tallest mountains, the Wasatch and Uinta Mountains, are part of the larger Rocky Mountain range. Most of the mountains are covered with forests that provide homes to many wild animals. There are so many fun things to do in Utah's mountains, such as camping, fishing, hunting, hiking, biking, and water and snow skiing, just to name a few!

Draw a picture of a scene from Utah's Rocky Mountain region.

THE NATIONAL PARKS

Utah is home to five national parks! Arches, Bryce Canyon, Canyonlands, Capitol Reef, and Zion National Parks can all be found in southern Utah. Imagine that you are planning a family trip to see one of the parks. Use this page to help you plan the trip. Visit www.nps.gov to help you learn more about the parks. You can find a park by state or by name. Do some research about all five parks before choosing the one you want to plan your trip for.

Amount of time needed to get to the park:

_____

Directions to the park:

_____

_____

_____

_____

Operating hours of the facilities during your visit:

_____

Available campground locations:

_____

_____

Where I want to camp:

_____

We will be visiting

_____

National Park.

Date(s) of your visit:

_____

Distance to park:

_____

NATIONAL PARK TIMELINE

UTAH

1900   1910   1920   1930

1919
Zion National Park

1928
Bryce Canyon
National Park

Different lengths of trails available:

_____

_____

_____

_____

_____

Things to do at the park:

_____

_____

_____

_____

Nearby attractions:

_____

_____

_____

Likely weather conditions:

_____

Some history of the park:

_____

_____

_____

_____

Some details of the nature and science of the park:

_____

_____

_____

_____

Fun things for kids to do in the park:

_____

_____

_____

_____

Things I'm looking forward to most:

_____

_____

_____

1964
Canyonlands
National Park

1950   1960   1970

1971
Arches National Park
Capitol Reef National Park

DO YOU KNOW YOUR NATIONAL PARKS?

Now that you have researched the five national parks in Utah and know all about them, fill in the blanks below with the correct park name.

1. _____ National Park is named for its stone arches that were created by flowing water and blowing wind wearing away holes in the soft rock over thousands of years.

2. The largest of Utah's parks is _____ National Park. It has deep gorges, huge rock towers, and three rivers (the Green, the Colorado, and the San Juan) run through it.

3. Set aside as protected land in 1919, _____ National Park is Utah's first park. It has beautiful canyons formed by the Virgin River.

4. Water has cut interesting shapes in the red sandstone cliffs of _____ National Park. Robbers Butch Cassidy and Sundance Kid used this park as a hideout.

5. _____ National Park's rocks were uniquely carved by wind, ice, and water. It is one of the most colorful parks in the world.

TOURISM IN UTAH

Tourism is a big industry in Utah. People come here to visit our forests, mountains, ski resorts, monuments, and state and national parks.

At www.travel.utah.gov you can learn all about our office of tourism and many of the tourist destinations in Utah. You can also go to www.visitutah.com to learn about tourist attractions. This office has chosen various slogans, or sayings, over the years to use in advertising. The point is to entice people to come visit Utah. Imagine that you have just been asked by the governor's office to come up with a new slogan and ad campaign for next year. Write and design your slogan below. It should be short and catchy. You should design it to look appealing, too.

FIELD TRIP: PARK CITY

Park City is known to be a tourist hangout in Utah. It is a historic mining town that now has multiple resorts, museums, concerts, summer and winter activities, and hosts the Sundance Film Festival. When you and your family make a day trip to Park City, pretend to be tourists and learn everything you can about the community. And, for a fun change of pace, watch the other tourists and see what they do and how they perceive the town.

What time of the year did you go Park City?

_____

What did you do while you were there?

_____

_____

_____

What were the tourists doing?

_____

_____

_____

Do you think some of the tourists might have been from another country?

_____

_____

_____

Draw some of the tourists you saw.

UTAH'S STATE & NATIONAL PARKS

Below is a map that shows all of Utah's state and national parks and national recreation areas, monuments, historic sites, and forests. Study the map and use the information to answer the questions.

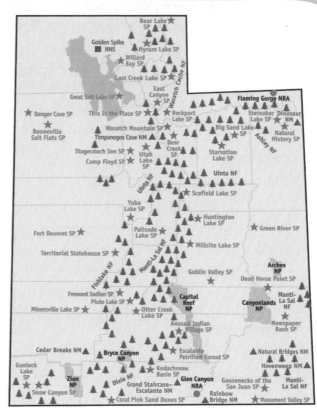

1. According to the map, does it look like Utah's lands are owned mostly by state or national government?

_____

2. What do you notice about the location of the national forests?

_____

_____

3. How many national recreation areas are there in our state?

_____

4. How many national monuments are there in our state?

_____

5. Describe the location of Danger Cave State Park.

_____

_____

6. Which locations on the map are closest to where you live?

_____

_____

LEGEND

★ State Park (SP)
● National Park (NP)
● National Recreation Area (NRA)
▲ National Monument (NM)
■ National Historic Site (NHS)
▲ National Forest (NF)

0 10 20 30 40 50
miles

THIS IS ONLY A DRILL

Living near Utah's mountains brings a lot of beauty and recreation opportunities to our state's citizens. The mountains also bring with them some dangers. One danger that we all need to be prepared for is an earthquake. Utah is a seismically active region. That means that the earth's plates below us move. Usually the movement is so minor we don't notice it. But often in Utah people feel earthquakes. We should always be prepared in case we have a big earthquake. Use this planner to help your family be prepared in the case of an earthquake.

Nearby emergency contact
(name and number):

_____

_____

Out-of-state emergency contact
(name and number):

_____

_____

Escape routes from each room in your home:

_____

_____

_____

_____

Meeting place in the neighborhood
(if you can't enter your home):

_____

_____

Meeting place in the region
(if you can't enter your neighborhood):

_____

_____

Emergency phone numbers
(other than 9-1-1):

Fire:

_____

Police:

_____

Hospital:

_____

Insurance information:

_____

_____

Install and check smoke detectors.
Check your smoke detectors every six
months. Check them the same two dates
each year so it's easier to remember.
Family members' birthdays are always
a good time to do it.
Dates:

_____

Locations:

_____

Install and check fire extinguishers.
Check your fire extinguishers once a
year. Set the same date each year so it's
easier to remember.
Date:

_____

Locations:

_____

Keep a first-aid kit.
Location:

_____

CPR and other first-aid training:

_____

_____

Check furniture and items hanging on
the wall that could fall in an earthquake.
Secure the items to the wall.

Prepare 72-hour kits for each member
of the family, and have them in a place
you can easily get to them in the case of
an emergency. Change out food items in
your kits once a year. Set the same date
each year so it's easier to remember.
Date:

_____

Location:

_____

Have water containers filled and stored
in case of emergency. It is a good idea to
have large barrels to keep at your house
as well as smaller containers that you
could take with you if you have to leave.
Keep these near your 72-hour kits.
Location:

_____

It's a good idea to keep important
paperwork together in a safe place so
you could grab it and take it with you if
you needed to leave.

Revisit your emergency plan often.
Dates to revisit plan:

_____

Make sure everyone in your family has
a copy of the emergency information
with them. You might want to keep it in
the glove box of each car, in wallets, or
back packs.

FIND THE HIDDEN TERM

There are some special things in Utah, and some of them were even chosen by school children who petitioned the state legislature. Unscramble each of the clue words below and fill in the boxes next to the words. Copy the letters that have a number under them to the lines with the same numbers at the bottom of this page to find the hidden term.

ALLOSAURUS   BLUE SPRUCE   BONNEVILLE CUTTHROAT TROUT   CALIFORNIA GULL
CHERRY   COPPER   HONEY BEE   ROCKY MOUNTAIN ELK
SEGO LILY   TOPAZ   UTAH, THIS IS THE PLACE   COAL

cykro touminan kel   _ _ _ _ _ _ _ _ _ _ _ _ _ _ _
                              7   8

focliirana lugl   _ _ _ _ _ _ _ _ _ _ _ _ _
                          10

voleebinnl totruhtac torut   _
                                                                   4

noyhe ebe   _ _ _ _ _ _ _
                    5

bule rescup   _ _ _ _ _ _ _ _ _ _
               9

ogse lyil   _ _ _ _ _ _ _ _
             1

cehrry   _ _ _ _ _ _

cola   _ _ _ _
              11

zotpa   _ _ _ _ _
         2

roeppc   _ _ _ _ _ _

luslaoruas   _ _ _ _ _ _ _ _ _ _
              3

tuha htsi si teh caple   _ _ _ _ _ _ _ _ _ _ _ _ _ _ _ _ _ _
                                          6   12

_ _ _ _ _ _ _ _ _ _ _ _
1 2 3 4 5 6 7 8 9 10 11 12

FAVORITE STATE SYMBOLS

Have an adult help you do an internet search about Utah's state symbols. Choose four of them that you find the most interesting. Write down each symbol you chose and three facts about each one. Then, draw a picture of each symbol.

SYMBOL: _____

Fact 1: _____

Fact 2: _____

Fact 3: _____

SYMBOL: _____

Fact 1: _____

Fact 2: _____

Fact 3: _____

SYMBOL: _____

Fact 1: _____

Fact 2: _____

Fact 3: _____

SYMBOL: _____

Fact 1: _____

Fact 2: _____

Fact 3: _____

PALEO-INDIANS

The first people to live here were Paleo-Indians. Paleo means ancient, or very old. Paleo-Indians lived all over the Americas. They hunted mammoths, mastodons, large wild cats, small horses, rabbits, antelope, and deer for food. They caught birds and fish. They gathered berries, nuts, seeds, and roots from plants. They didn't live in one place, but moved around to hunt and gather food. Compare how the Paleo-Indians lived to how you live today. In the left section, fill in details of how the Paleo-Indians lived. In the right section, fill in details of how you live. In the middle, fill in details that are the same for how both the Paleo-Indians and you live.

PALEO-INDIANS

BOTH

ME

ARCHAIC INDIANS

As the climate changed, so did the people's way of life. The people who lived during this time are called Archaic Indians. Archaic means old. Many of the giant animals no longer lived on the Earth. The people hunted deer and birds for food. They made new tools that allowed them to hunt smaller, faster animals. They also began to plant crops because they didn't move around as much as the people before them. To store the food for winter, they dug pits in the ground. Compare how the Archaic Indians lived to how you live today. In the left section, fill in details of how the Archaic Indians lived. In the right, fill in details of how you live. In the middle, fill in details that are the same for how both the Archaic Indians and you live.

ARCHAIC INDIANS

BOTH

ME

ARCHAIC AND PALEO-INDIANS

You know how your way of life compares to those who lived here long ago. But how do two groups from long ago compare to one another? Compare how the Paleo-Indians lived with how the Archaic Indians lived. In the left section, fill in details of how the Paleo-Indians lived. In the right section, fill in details of how the Archaic Indians lived. In the middle section, fill in details that are the same for both groups.

PALEO-INDIANS   BOTH   ARCHAIC INDIANS

What were some of the major differences between the two groups?

_____

_____

_____

STUDY ROCK ART

As time went on, some Archaic Indians left the area that is now Utah. Those who stayed mixed with two new groups that moved here: the Ancestral Puebloans and the Fremont. The Ancestral Puebloans people are known for their rock art. Everywhere they lived, they painted and carved pictures on canyon walls. The pictures tell stories, and they are sacred to native people today.

What symbols can you recognize in the rock art?

_____

_____

What symbols might be related to medicine and healing? Spirituality?

_____

_____

Choose three of the symbols and write what you think they could represent.

_____

_____

_____

_____

Why do you think native people chose rock art as a way to record their stories?

_____

_____

_____

_____

FIELD TRIP: ZION CANYON NATIONAL PARK PETROGLYPHS

Zion Canyon National Park has several petroglyph sites at the park. Unfortunately, some of them are no longer made public because of damage caused by people. The ancient rock art needs to be treated just like art in museums—no touching!

It is possible to see some of the petroglyphs and pictographs at the park. The best way is to stop by the Zion Canyon Visitor Center for information. Talk to the park rangers there and they will tell you which sites you can see and how to locate them.

What exactly are petroglyphs and pictographs? What are the differences between the two terms? Use a dictionary to look up the words and then write the definitions.

Petroglyph: _____

_____

Pictograph: _____

Draw pictures of some of the rock art you saw during your visit to Zion Canyon.

• ZION CANYON •

GEOGRAPHY & SOCIAL STUDIES

MAKE YOUR OWN ROCK ART

You can make your very own rock art with just a few ingredients from the craft store and the help of an adult.

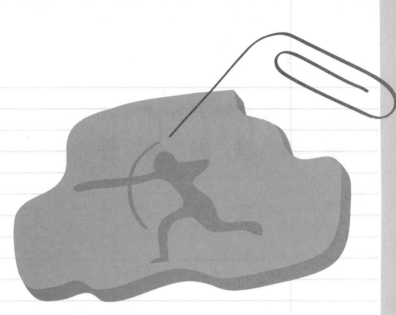

WHAT YOU WILL NEED:

plaster
cookie sheet
wax paper
spatula
dark orange craft paint
paper clips

WHAT TO DO:

1. Mix the plaster, following the instructions on the package.

2. Line your cookie sheet with wax paper.

3. Poor the plaster into the cookie sheet. Use a flat spatula to spread it out on the cookie sheet. Let the plaster dry overnight.

4. Paint the entire surface of the plaster with a color similar to that of the red rock cliffs of Utah. Let the paint dry a few hours.

5. Have an adult use a blunt object, such as a butter knife, to break up the plaster into smaller pieces to make rocks.

6. Unwind the end of a paper clip. Use the end to carve symbols into your rocks. What story will you tell with your rock art?

7. Share your rock art with others to see if they can guess the meaning of your symbols.

SOLVE AN ANCIENT MYSTERY

The Ancestral Puebloans lived in the Colorado Plateau for over a thousand years. Then they left their homes and moved on. Did they have enemies close by who attacked? Did they find better land? Stories passed down say they might have found new lands for religious reasons. No one knows for sure. Today you get a chance to finish their story. You decide why the Ancestral Puebloans might have left this region. Tell the story in your own words below.

GEOGRAPHY & SOCIAL STUDIES

UTAH'S FIVE TRIBES

Utah has five historic tribes: the Goshute, Shoshone, Navajo, Paiute, and Ute tribes. They are known as historic tribes because we have written information about their history and way of life from hundreds of years ago. Although these are historic tribes, they still exist today. In the reading section (pages 147-157) of this book, you learn about the cultures of these historic tribes. A good way to learn about the way of life of the tribes today is to visit their websites.

Visit each of the tribes' websites to learn more about the history of teach tribe and to learn about how the tribe functions today. Take notes on the things you find most interesting.

Goshute Tribe
www.goshutetribe.com

Shoshone Tribe
www.shoshoneindian.com

Navajo Tribe
www.navajo-nsn.gov

Paiute Tribe
www.utahpaiutes.org

Ute Tribe
www.utetribe.com

INDIAN TRIBAL LANDS

This map shows where Utah's historic tribes were found in Utah and where you can find their reservations today.

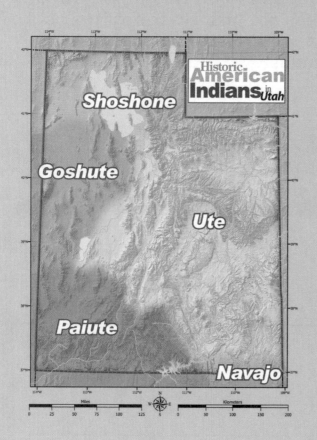

Historic American Indians in Utah

Shoshone
Goshute
Ute
Paiute
Navajo

Which tribe covered the largest area in Utah?

_____

Which tribe covered the smallest area in Utah?

_____

Which tribe was found in the driest area?

_____

Which tribe lived in the region with the most rivers to travel on and fish in?

_____

Which tribes had to be prepared for cold winters?

_____

_____

_____

Which tribes had very mountainous terrain to travel across?

_____

_____

Think about what you know of Utah's land. Using that information, what conclusions can you make about what life was like where each tribe lived?

_____

_____

_____

_____

_____

NATURAL DYES

The first people to live in Utah, the American Indians, lived off of the earth. They found many uses for plants. One of the uses was using plants to dye string, cloth, and other things. You can try using plants as dyes with the help of an adult. Here is a list of some plants you can use and how long to boil each in a pot of water before you can use it as a dye. Try this out on some string or a small piece of cloth. If it works well, you may want to try it on some other items.

Sample list of dyes and sources:

Barks: Boil one hour
BROWN—ash, birch, walnut, maple
BLACK—alder
GOLD—eucalyptus
RED—bayberry

Twigs and Leaves: Boil two hours
GRAY—blackberry plant
YELLOW—poplar leaves, peach leaves
LIME GREEN—lily of the valley leaves

Vegetables and Berries: Boil 45 minutes
RED—raspberries, beets, strawberries
BLUE—blueberries, boysenberries
YELLOW—onion skin
GREEN—spinach, squash
BROWN—coffee grounds
ORANGE—carrots

Flowers: Boil 15 minutes
GREEN—morning glory
BEIGE—red bougainvillea
BLUE—cornflower, larkspur
RED—bloodroot poppy
YELLOW—goldenrod, dahlia, marguerite

PRESERVING MEAT

The Shoshone hunted buffalo, using its meat as a main source of food. To make it last longer, they dried it in the sun and made jerky, a meat that has been preserved through a process of drying. With the help of an adult, you can make your own jerky!

Ingredients:
LEAN MEAT AND SEASONING SALT

Directions:
1. Put the meat in the freezer until partially frozen. Partially frozen meat is easier to slice.

2. Slice meat thinly along the grain. Remove any visible fat.

3. Lay sliced meat on wax paper and sprinkle with seasoning salt. Work seasoning into the meat.

4. Put seasoned meat on a cookie sheet and place in the oven. Set oven temperature to 150 degrees. Cook for 5 hours. Leave the oven door slightly open to allow the water that is released from the meat to escape.

5. Allow the cooked meat to sit overnight before eating.

FIND THE INDIAN PEOPLES WORD SEARCH

Circle the names of Indian peoples in the word search puzzle.

ANCESTRAL PUEBLOANS	ARCHAIC INDIANS	GOSHUTE	NAVAJO
PAIUTE	PALEO-INDIANS	SHOSHONE	UTE

```
J  I  C  L  F  S  H  E  T  L  H  O  K  G  Z  W  U  I  P  F
V  A  M  R  E  I  X  J  D  C  S  Y  T  U  K  P  R  A  O  O
U  W  Y  R  X  I  M  P  N  M  F  B  Q  F  C  I  I  G  J  F
S  B  Q  R  X  B  J  M  R  L  F  G  P  A  S  U  D  A  A  Z
A  R  C  H  A  I  C  I  N  D  I  A  N  S  T  E  V  L  H  W
T  F  A  S  C  R  E  U  Q  G  K  N  H  E  N  A  A  E  G  I
G  O  F  N  V  Q  G  Q  S  J  E  B  G  O  N  Y  G  R  C  Q
Y  Q  Z  H  R  O  P  H  T  N  C  I  H  M  I  G  K  R  T  A
F  G  J  M  S  G  E  L  U  S  A  S  Q  W  M  C  O  A  L  J
U  W  T  H  U  B  A  L  L  Z  O  I  M  L  N  X  O  B  J  M
R  G  U  G  T  R  R  Z  H  H  D  A  D  A  G  B  R  S  H  F
D  T  C  B  E  A  J  S  Y  K  L  X  N  X  F  H  B  W  W  K
E  L  K  J  J  M  T  G  I  H  R  U  C  W  I  L  D  F  G  H
T  C  T  S  G  P  H  B  P  V  G  N  G  Z  K  O  E  Y  X  A
P  I  H  K  C  F  S  N  B  S  K  B  T  Z  T  O  E  V  B  Q
W  C  H  X  F  E  H  N  V  D  V  T  F  G  D  F  P  L  Q  L
A  N  C  E  S  T  R  A  L  P  U  E  B  L  O  A  N  S  A  A
H  P  V  L  R  Y  O  F  R  Z  N  E  J  N  E  Q  Y  F  J  P
Q  Q  D  Q  Z  L  P  V  S  M  H  V  V  Y  M  N  H  K  T  Z
E  A  S  I  B  D  C  Z  W  M  D  E  S  X  B  W  E  B  C  L
```

WHICH WAY DID HE GO?

In the 1500s, explorers from Spain and other countries in Europe began coming to the Americas. Eventually, explorers made their way inland towards Utah. This map shows some famous expeditions. The explorers took notes, drew maps, and gathered information about the region that they passed along to others when they returned home. Study the map and answer the questions.

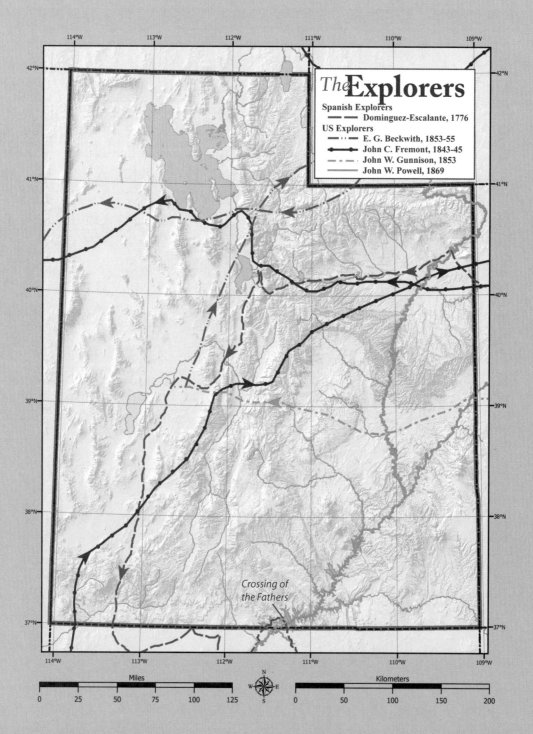

The **Explorers**

Spanish Explorers
— — Dominguez-Escalante, 1776

US Explorers
—··— E. G. Beckwith, 1853-55
—•— John C. Fremont, 1843-45
—·— John W. Gunnison, 1853
—— John W. Powell, 1869

Crossing of the Fathers

Miles
0   25   50   75   100   125

Kilometers
0   50   100   150   200

1. Follow John C. Fremont's route that starts in southern Utah. What does it look like happens off the map in Colorado?

_____

2. Why do you think John W. Gunnison's trail looks like it disappears when it reaches the Dominguez-Escalante trail?

_____

_____

3. Which region appears to be explored the least? Why do you think that is?

_____

_____

4. Which region appears to be explored the most? Why do you think that is?

_____

_____

5. Follow John W. Powell's route. Do you know what is significant about where his route goes in southern Utah?

_____

_____

6. Which of the routes are near where you live? What might have been the first thing the explorers noticed about the area where you live? What might they have liked or disliked?

_____

_____

_____

Trick question: It was impossible for there to have been any U.S. explorers or explorations before 1776. Do you know why that is?

_____

TRAPPER ROUTES

Much like the explorers, the trappers (people who catch animals in traps) made note of important information in the region as they passed through. They also passed along the information to others.

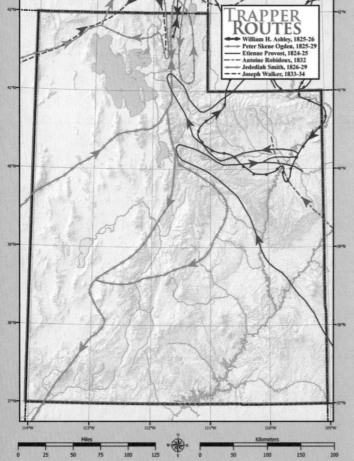

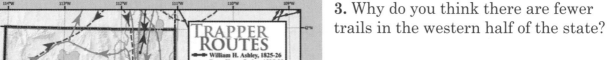

1. Which trappers never made it to the southern part of the state?

_____

_____

2. Around which landforms do most of the trails appear to follow?

_____

_____

3. Why do you think there are fewer trails in the western half of the state?

_____

_____

_____

4. Which trapper was the first to begin trapping in Utah?

_____

5. Which trapper was the last to begin trapping in Utah?

_____

6. Do you know which of these trappers have cities in Utah named after them?

_____

_____

GEOGRAPHY & SOCIAL STUDIES

FACT OR FICTION?

Some books say that mountain men were daring, tough adventurers. They say they fought Indians and bears at every turn. That is only partly true. Can you separate fact from fiction about mountain men? Take your best guess at which of these statements about mountain men are true.

Many mountain men were married, some to Indian women.

TRUE   FALSE

Their wives and families did not travel with them.

TRUE   FALSE

Most trapped for only a few years. Then they became guides, ranchers, farmers, or store owners.

TRUE   FALSE

They traveled by horse, mule, or canoe.

TRUE   FALSE

Most died from attack by wild animals.

TRUE   FALSE

Trapping was a hobby. Trappers did it purely for the excitement.

TRUE   FALSE

Mountain men were the best of the best all around. They were all brave, creative, and hardworking.

TRUE   FALSE

They often did not understand American Indians. Instead of respecting them, some saw them as people who were just in the way.

TRUE   FALSE

When beaver hats in the United States and in Europe went out of style, the fur trade ended and many mountain men had to find new ways to make money.

TRUE   FALSE

ALWAYS GROWING AND CHANGING

When the Mormon pioneers first came to this area, the land was owned by Mexico. A year after the pioneers arrived, the land changed hands. In a war with Mexico, the United States won a huge piece of the West, including Utah. The U.S. government set up the Utah Territory.

Many other people started coming to Utah to settle. People passing through to California sometimes stopped to spend the winter in Utah. Jewish people began moving to Utah. In fact, Jewish merchants opened the first store on Main Street in Salt Lake City. U.S. soldiers came to Utah both to protect the settlers from Indians and to make sure the settlers were obeying U.S. laws. Mormon converts from Europe sailed to the United States and traveled west to Utah.

Write about the different people who make up your community today. Fill in the blank boxes. You might have people of different religions, different family make-ups, different levels of education, different ages, and people of countless other differences. Diversity helps make our state great!

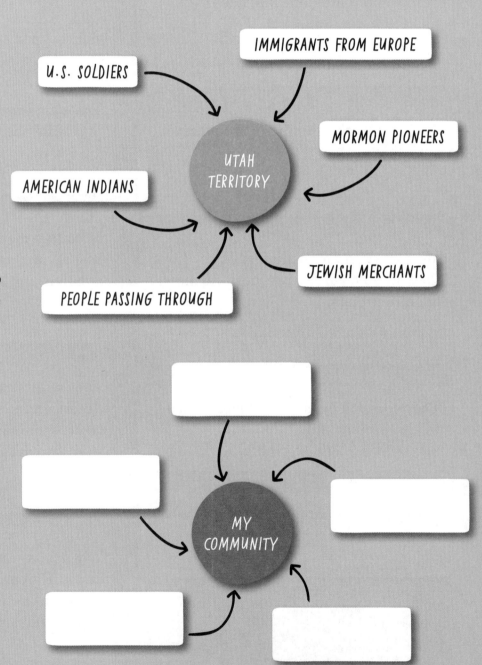

U.S. SOLDIERS

IMMIGRANTS FROM EUROPE

MORMON PIONEERS

AMERICAN INDIANS

UTAH TERRITORY

JEWISH MERCHANTS

PEOPLE PASSING THROUGH

MY COMMUNITY

MIGRATION MAZE

Help the immigrants find Utah by drawing a path for them to follow in the maze.

READING & WRITING

NAMESAKE

If Utah's lakes and rivers could talk, they would have many stories to tell. Each place and land feature in Utah has a story behind its name. Panguitch Lake is a Paiute Indian name for "water with plenty of fish." Posey Lake, Chepeta Lake, and Peteetneet Creek were all named after Ute Indian leaders. The Colorado River might tell you it has had many names. One came from Mojave Indians, one from the Spanish, and one from people who came to Utah later. The Green River has a similar story. It was first named Rio Verde. That means "green river" in Spanish. Shoshone Indians called it Seeds-kee-dee-agie, or "Prairie Hen River." Indians, Spanish explorers, fur trappers, U.S. explorers, farmers, miners, and railroad workers have all walked its banks. The Great Salt Lake might tell you that people once thought it was part of the Pacific Ocean. They thought that because the water is salty like the ocean.

What about you? What is your namesake, or where did your name come from? Write an informative paragraph sharing the history of your name.

CHALLENGE!

TOPIC SENTENCE: Explain that you will be sharing where your name came from.

_____

SUPPORTING SENTENCE 1: Begin explaining your namesake.

_____

SUPPORTING SENTENCE 2: More information on your namesake.

_____

SUPPORTING SENTENCE 3: More information on your namesake.

_____

CONCLUDING SENTENCE: Restate and wrap up the purpose of the paragraph.

_____

Do you have more to say about your name? Use the information from the previous page as an introductory paragraph and continue working on a five-paragraph essay. Tell as much as you can about your namesake.

INTRODUCTORY PARAGRAPH

_____

_____

_____

_____

SUPPORTING DETAILS (USE SUPPORTING SENTENCE 1)	SUPPORTING DETAILS (USE SUPPORTING SENTENCE 2)	SUPPORTING DETAILS (USE SUPPORTING SENTENCE 3)
_____	_____	_____
_____	_____	_____
_____	_____	_____
_____	_____	_____
_____	_____	_____

CONCLUDING PARAGRAPH

_____

_____

_____

_____

LAND METAPHORS

A metaphor is a word or phrase for one thing that is used to refer to another thing. Writers use metaphors to add emotion and feeling. One writer, Barry Lopez, wrote,

"To put your hands in a river is to feel the chords that bind the earth together."

His metaphor relates rivers to chords. A chord is three or more musical tones sounded at the same time. His metaphor paints an image in our minds of rivers all around the world playing musical notes together, their beautiful music binding the earth.

Think of a time you spent outdoors in Utah. What land feature stuck out most to you? Choose one of the land features below and write a sentence or two describing the feature using a metaphor. What will you relate the landform to in your metaphor?

MOUNTAIN	VALLEY	BASIN	PLATEAU	LAKE	RIVER	STREAM

_____

_____

_____

_____

Can you think of second land feature metaphor?

_____

_____

_____

_____

Draw pictures of the land features you wrote about to show how you visualize your metaphors.

CITE TEXT EVIDENCE: ANCIENT LAKE BONNEVILLE

Did you know that a lake once covered much of Utah? Read about the ancient lake and answer the questions.

1. Long ago, the weather in Utah was much colder than it is now. The snow and ice just kept piling up. Long, thick layers covered the mountains in the north.

2. Then slowly the climate got warmer. The glaciers began to melt. As they melted, they began to move. They took dirt and rocks with them. They carved canyons and valleys in Utah's mountains. This kind of erosion created Little Cottonwood Canyon, near Salt Lake City.

3. The water ran down the canyons into a growing lake. It was called Lake Bonneville. The huge lake spread over the Great Basin. It spread through canyons and surrounding valleys. It covered much of western Utah. It was over 1,000 feet deep!

4. After a long time, the water overflowed into what is now Idaho. It joined the Snake and Columbia rivers. From there it rolled to the Pacific Ocean.

5. The lake was still here, but it was not as deep. Its waves washed against the sides of the Wasatch Mountains. They formed a bench, or terrace. Look at the benches today. You can see where the shoreline of this ancient lake once was.

6. Mountain streams flowed down to the lake. They carried loads of sediment. As the streams entered the lake, they slowed down. They spread out. They dropped the rich mountain soil and gravel they carried. These areas now have some of the best soil in the state.

7. The climate continued to change. In time, Lake Bonneville dried up. The Great Salt Lake, Utah Lake, and Sevier Lake are all that is left of the ancient lake today.

How was Lake Bonneville created?
In which paragraph(s) did you find
the answer? Start your answer, "In
paragraph ____ it said . . ."

_____

_____

_____

Describe Lake Bonneville. In which
paragraph(s) did you gather these details?

_____

_____

_____

Red Rock Pass

Sevier
Desert

Sevier River

MAP KEY

Lake Bonneville

Today's lakes

N
NW   NE
W   E
SW   SE
S

0 10 20 30 40 50
miles

What evidence do we have today that a lake once covered Utah? In which paragraph(s)
did you gather these details?

_____

_____

_____

What do the Great Salt Lake, Utah Lake, and Sevier Lake have in common? Which
sentence in the text helps you answer this question?

_____

_____

_____

_____

THREE TYPES OF COMMUNITIES

You can find three kinds of communities around the state: rural, suburban, and urban. Read about each kind of community and do the activities that follow.

Urban Communities

Cities are busy places. They have sidewalks full of people. The streets are noisy with cars. There are houses, apartments, and rows of businesses. This kind of community is called urban. People in urban areas often walk or ride buses or trains to get from place to place. Utah's most urban area is Salt Lake City.

Suburban Communities

Some people like to live outside the city. There the houses and businesses are more spread out. There are parks and lawns to play on. These areas are called suburbs. Many people work in the cities but live in the suburbs. They drive or take commuter trains to work. To commute means to travel some distance between home and work. Along the Wasatch Front, people ride TRAX. TRAX is a light rail system that carries people to and from the city.

Suburbs are often built on land that was once farmland. About 100 years ago, people built Utah's first suburbs. They were called "streetcar suburbs" because they were built at the end of streetcar lines. People could live outside the city and ride the streetcars to work. Some early streetcar suburbs of Salt Lake City were Highland Park, Sugar House, Federal Heights, and Forest Dale.

After cars were invented, more people moved to the suburbs. They could drive from home to work. New suburbs outside of Salt Lake City included Rose Park and Glendale. Suburbs are still being built today. One new suburb in the Salt Lake Valley is called Daybreak.

Rural Communities

Some people live in small towns or on farms in the country. Farmers need plenty of land to grow crops and as pasture for their livestock. This kind of open land is rural. Rural areas look very different from urban areas.

Most Utahns live in urban areas and suburbs, but many prefer rural areas. Except for the Wasatch Front (from Logan to Provo), most of Utah is rural.

READING & WRITING

Do you live in an urban, suburban, or rural community? Draw a picture of where you live. Then write a descriptive paragraph about what type of community you live in. Include details that make it urban, suburban, or rural. Use the lines below to form your ideas and then write your paragraph on the next page.

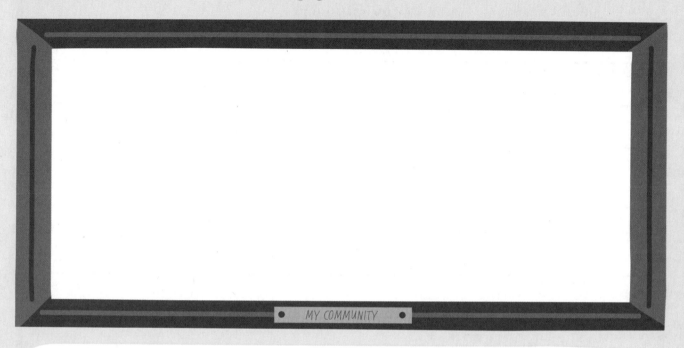

MY COMMUNITY

TOPIC SENTENCE: State which type or community you live in and give your city or town name.

_____

SUPPORTING SENTENCE 1: Describe one of your city/town's traits that make that type of community.

_____

SUPPORTING SENTENCE 2: Describe another of your city/town's traits that make that type of community.

_____

SUPPORTING SENTENCE 3: Describe one more of your city/town's traits that make that type of community.

_____

CONCLUDING SENTENCE: Restate which kind of community you live in.

_____

MY COMMUNITY

_____

_____

_____

_____

_____

_____

_____

_____

_____

_____

_____

_____

_____

_____

_____

_____

FIELD TRIP: SALT LAKE CITY

Ask your parents or an adult friend to take you to Salt Lake City. Even if you already live there, try to see the city differently than you usually do as you drive around the area. Salt Lake City is definitely an urban community.

Maybe you can walk around downtown. List some things that make Salt Lake City an urban community.

_____

_____

_____

_____

As you drive around the city, what things do you notice that are different from a suburban or rural community?

_____

_____

_____

_____

What are some positive things about living in a city? What are some negative things?

_____

_____

_____

_____

HEAR, HEAR! THIS IS THE BEST!

An opinion is a belief or way of thinking about something. When good writers share their opinions, they have reasons that support or explain their opinion. Let's practice writing an opinion with supporting reasons.

In your opinion, which type of community is the best to live in: rural, suburban, or urban? Use this organizer to help you organize your ideas. In this step of the writing process, we are just organizing ideas, not using complete sentences yet; words or phrases are okay to use here.

INTRODUCTION

Answer to the question:

Three supporting reasons:

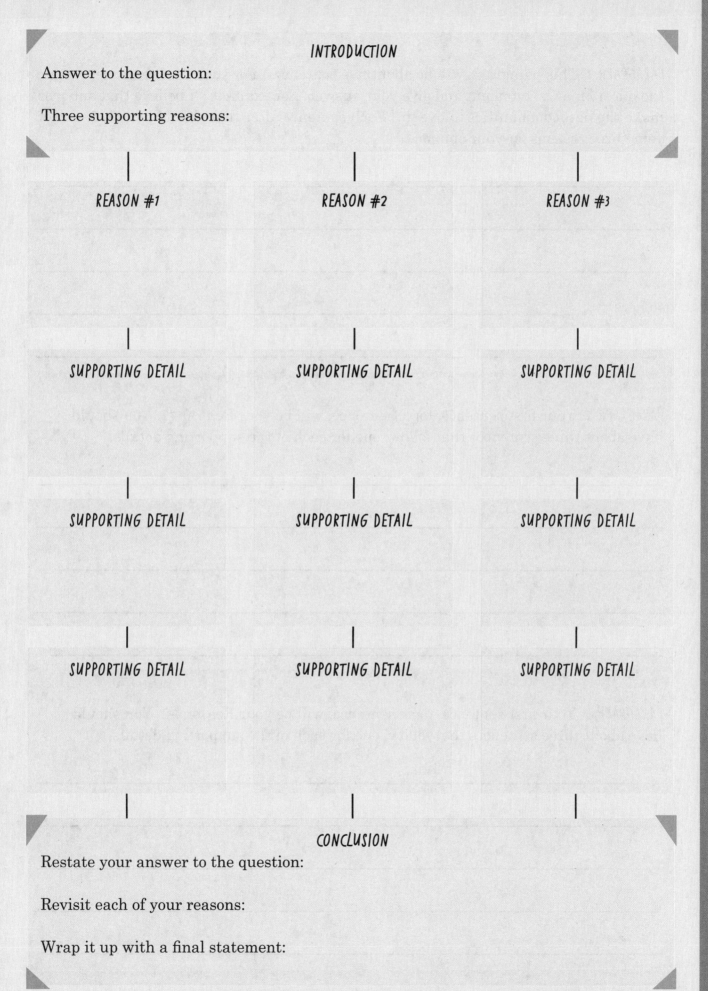

REASON #1	REASON #2	REASON #3
SUPPORTING DETAIL	SUPPORTING DETAIL	SUPPORTING DETAIL
SUPPORTING DETAIL	SUPPORTING DETAIL	SUPPORTING DETAIL
SUPPORTING DETAIL	SUPPORTING DETAIL	SUPPORTING DETAIL

CONCLUSION

Restate your answer to the question:

Revisit each of your reasons:

Wrap it up with a final statement:

PARAGRAPH 1: This paragraph will be about five sentences. For your first sentence, restate the question as a statement and give your answer. For example, "I believe that suburbs make the best communities to live in." Each sentence after that should introduce one of your three reasons for your opinion.

_____

_____

_____

_____

PARAGRAPH 2: Your first sentence, topic sentence, will be your Reason #1. You should have about three sentences that follow, one for each of the supporting details.

_____

_____

_____

_____

PARAGRAPH 3: Your first sentence, topic sentence, will be your Reason #2. You should have about three sentences that follow, one for each of the supporting details.

_____

_____

_____

_____

PARAGRAPH 4: Your first sentence, topic sentence, will be your Reason #3. You should have about three sentences that follow, one for each of the supporting details.

_____

_____

_____

_____

PARAGRAPH 5: This paragraph will be about five sentences. For your first sentence, you will again restate the question as a statement and give your answer. Each sentence after that should restate/revisit each of your reasons. Be careful not to introduce any new information here! Your last sentence should wrap up all of your writing.

_____

_____

_____

_____

_____

_____

_____

_____

THIS IS OUR PLACE!

People have a lot to think about when they decide where to live. Some common things people have to think about are where their job is located, where family is located, what the weather is like, what the land is like, and which type of community they want to live in. How did your family decide where to live? Use this page to help you research and write about how your family chose where to live.

Which type of community do you live in?

☐ SUBURBAN   ☐ URBAN   ☐ RURAL

Where did your family live before?

_____

Why did your family move from the previous location?

_____

Do you have family nearby?

_____

Where do your parents work?

_____

_____

Write a paragraph summarizing all of the reasons why your family chose to live where they do now. Your first sentence should be your topic sentence that introduces where your family lives now. You should write one sentence for each of the reasons why you live there. Your last sentence should wrap up your paragraph by restating where you live now.

_____

_____

_____

_____

_____

_____

MY FAVORITE PLACE!

Utah is full of wonderful places, from the red rock cliffs of the south to the tall white snowy peaks of the north. Where is your favorite place in Utah? Write about your favorite place. Be sure to include details about where the place is, when you were last there, what you do there, and what it sounds and looks like there. Write away!

_____

_____

_____

_____

_____

_____

_____

_____

_____

_____

_____

_____

Utah's natural resources make it a logical place for certain job industries. Mining, oil, agriculture, tourism, skiing, and fishing are all big industries here.

Imagine that you work for a local newspaper and have been asked to write help wanted ads. Choose three industries that appeal most to you. Write an ad for each, telling all about the industry and enticing people to apply for the job. Include a catchy title and information about the kind of job that is available. If you need some ideas, look at the employment section of your newspaper, or at the website of your local paper and search for jobs.

HELP WANTED!

_____

_____

_____

_____

_____

HELP WANTED!

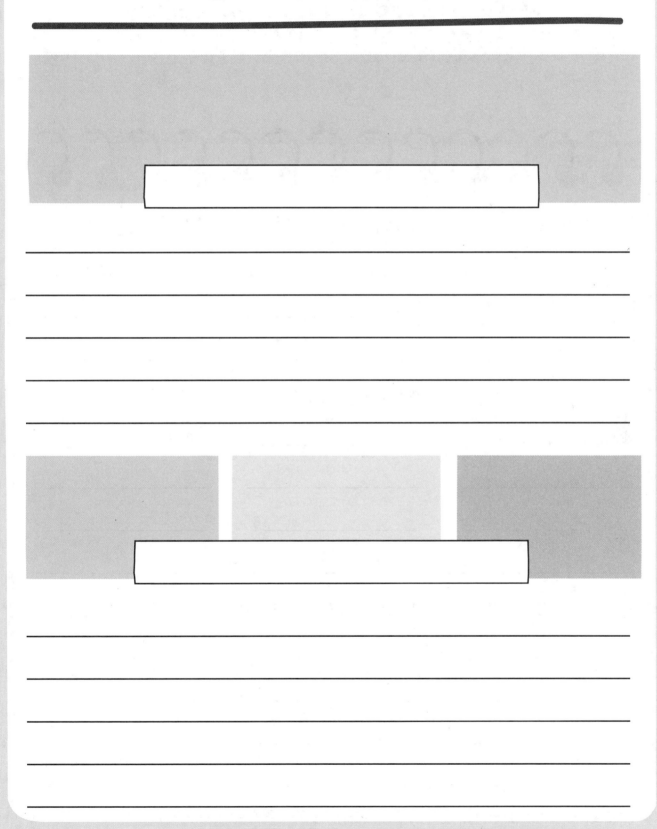

FRONT-PAGE NEWS!

Some people used to think that sea monsters lived in Utah's Great Salt Lake, and others thought the lake may contain whales. Imagine something has just been spotted in the lake by many people! What is it? Is it friendly? Use this page to help you plan your front-page news article.

WHO HAS SPOTTED SOMETHING?

_____

_____

_____

WHAT HAS HAPPENED? WHAT CHANGES HAS IT CAUSED?

_____

_____

_____

WHERE DID THIS HAPPEN?

_____

_____

_____

WHEN DID THIS HAPPEN?

_____

_____

_____

WHY DID THIS HAPPEN?

_____

WHY IS THIS IMPORTANT?

_____

_____

_____

HOW DID THIS HAPPEN?

_____

_____

_____

HOW HAS THIS AFFECTED PEOPLE?

_____

_____

_____

_____

Now write your news article. Be sure to include:
- An introductory paragraph where you give an overview of what is happening.
- A paragraph for each detail you want to give more information about.
- A closing paragraph wrapping up what information has been shared.

NEWS

THE GREAT DEBATE: LAKE POWELL

When Glen Canyon Dam was built, it formed Lake Powell. We gained a beautiful lake with fun things to do. We also gained a way to make electricity. In the process, we lost some important things, too. The water buried rock formations, some animal habitats, and American Indian rock art.

Some people think the lake should be drained. They want us to see the beauty of those rocks and cliffs and to return things to the way they were before. What do you think?

Before you make a decision, it's always a good idea to do more research. Ask other people about their experiences with Lake Powell. Do some reading on history or other reputable Internet sites.

In one paragraph, share your opinion. Your first sentence should introduce your opinion. The following sentences should state your reasons. Since this is just a paragraph, have your last sentence restate your opinion to wrap it up.

_____

_____

_____

_____

_____

_____

_____

FIELD TRIP: LAKE POWELL

Now that you have done some research about Lake Powell, see if your family can take a short vacation to the lake. Have a great time playing, boating, water skiing, camping, or whatever else your family enjoys.

While you are there, take a few minutes to notice the beauty of the red rocks and the location of the lake. Maybe you can see Glen Canyon Dam.

In your research for the activity on the previous page you formed an opinion about draining the lake. Did your opinion change after your visit? Why or why not? Explain below.

_____

_____

_____

_____

_____

_____

_____

_____

_____

_____

_____

NATIONAL PARKS

An important reading skill is being able to reference exactly what the text said to answer questions about the text. Read this informational text about Utah's national parks. Then determine in which line or lines you find the answer to each question. Finally, answer each question.

1. Many places in Utah are unusual and beautiful. They have been made into special
2. parks and monuments. The government pays park rangers to take care of the state
3. and national parks.
4. Zion National Park was Utah's first national park. It was set aside as protected land
5. in 1919. For thousands of years, the Virgin River has flowed through the rock. It has
6. carved beautiful canyons. The first people to live there were Ancestral Puebloan
7. Indians. Later, Southern Paiutes moved in. They were living there when the Mormon
8. pioneers arrived in Utah.
9. Canyonlands National Park is the largest of Utah's parks. It has deep gorges and
10. huge rock towers. Our three major rivers run through it—the Green, the
11. Colorado, and the San Juan. Fremont Indians once hunted in Canyonlands.
12. Later, the Ancestral Puebloans farmed there. You can see ruins and rock art on
13. the canyon walls.
14. Capitol Reef National Park has red sandstone cliffs. Water has cut strange
15. shapes in the rocks. Rock art shows us that American Indians lived there for
16. many years. Robbers Butch Cassidy and the Sundance Kid used Capitol Reef as
17. a hideout.
18. Arches National Park is named for its stone arches. The rocks are mainly
19. pink sandstone. A stream of water can wear a hole in this soft rock. Blowing
20. sand can also wear a hole through the rock. This takes thousands of years, and
21. it is still going on. Long ago, American Indians lived among the arches and
22. painted rock art there.
23. Bryce Canyon National Park is one of the most colorful parks in the world.
24. White, yellow, red, orange, and purple rocks blend together. Wind, ice, and
25. water carved the rocks into many shapes. The park was named after Ebenezer
26. Bryce, an early rancher. He once looked into the deep canyon and said, "This is
27. no place to lose a cow!"

LINE #   Who takes care of the national parks?

_____   _____

What was Utah's first national park?

_____   _____

Which groups of people have lived in the area that is now Zion National Park?

_____   _____

What are some of the physical features of Canyonlands National Park?

_____   _____

Describe some of the history of the area that is now Canyonlands National Park?

_____   _____

What might the ruins and rock art in the Canyonlands be from? Use some information from the text and knowledge that you have to form your answer.

_____   _____

How do we know that American Indians lived for many years in the area that is now Capitol Reef National Park?

_____   _____

How did Arches National Park get its name?

_____   _____

What is unique about Bryce Canyon National Park?

_____   _____

How did the rocks in Bryce Canyon become so oddly shaped?

_____   _____

THE VIEW FROM HERE

Utah has many natural wonders and so much beauty. Write a description of one of your favorite natural beauties in Utah. It might be near your home or somewhere you have visited. A good description appeals to the senses. Be sure to write what you see, hear, smell, feel, and even taste at this place.

⭐ One of my favorite places of natural beauty in Utah is . . . _____

WHAT IT LOOKS LIKE

_____

WHAT IT SOUNDS LIKE

_____

WHAT IT SMELLS LIKE

_____

WHAT IT FEELS LIKE

_____

WHAT IT TASTES LIKE

_____

TRUE RED? OR TRUE BLUE?

It all started with a baseball game in 1895. Stories say neither team scored, and the game ended in a pretty rough fight. Just who were these rivals? Brigham Young University and the University of Utah. They may not be in the same conference anymore, but the rivalry lives on for many people in Utah!

Do you bleed red or blue? Find out how many people in your life bleed red and how many bleed blue. Tally how many people root for each team and their reasons for their choice.

The number of people who bleed red for the U of U (put a tally mark for each person):	The number of people who bleed blue for BYU (put a tally mark for each person):
Why people bleed red:	Why people bleed blue:

FIELD TRIP: VISIT THE U AND BYU

Take a trip to both the University of Utah and Brigham Young University and walk around the campuses. You will need to plan two separate days for this field trip. Talk to students you see and ask them how they enjoy going to school there. Do you already know someone who is a student at one of these universities? Talk to them before you go to the schools if you can.

Using data from your observations and what students told you about the universities, make two lists for each school—a positive, or pro, list and a negative, or con, list and fill in your information.

UNIVERSITY OF UTAH

BRIGHAM YOUNG UNIVERSITY

PROS

_____

_____

_____

_____

CONS

_____

_____

_____

PROS

_____

_____

_____

_____

CONS

_____

_____

_____

Which school do you think you might like to attend when you go to college?

_____

FIVE HISTORIC TRIBES

In the 1700s, people other than native Indians began coming to Utah. The first people were Spanish explorers then came Catholic priests. Later, fur trappers and U.S. explorers, and then Mormon pioneers came. These groups all wrote diaries, letters, and reports about the native Indians who were here at that time. These things all tell of the history of the native people. That is why they are known as historic Indians. The five historic tribes are the Goshute, Shoshone, Navajo, Paiute, and Ute tribes. Read about each of these tribes. Then take notes by filling in the chart at the end of each section.

SHOSHONE

The Shoshone believe the Fremont people were their ancestors. An ancestor is a relative who came before you. The Shoshone called themselves Nimi.

The Shoshone moved with the seasons. They hunted and gathered in the mountains and valleys of northern Utah. They were not full-time farmers, but they planted seeds from some wild plants. They ground seeds and nuts into flour. Their ancestors had done this for hundreds of years, and we still do it today. They made the flour into cakes and baked them.

The Shoshone made baskets out of plant leaves and stems. They also made water jugs.

Buffalo and Tipis

The Shoshone hunted buffalo that roamed in the valleys. They used every part of the buffalo. The meat was a main source of food. They cooked it over an open fire with vegetables such as corn.

To make it last longer, they dried it in the sun and made jerky.

The Shoshone lived in villages, like the Ute, Paiute, and Goshute. The tribe was divided into smaller groups called bands.

The Shoshone built two types of homes. One type was a shade house. They placed green leafy branches over a framework of wooden poles. They used willows, quaking aspen branches, reeds, and tall grasses to make them.

The Shoshone also built tipis (TEE peez). They made a frame of wooden poles and then stretched buffalo hides around it. The Shoshone were known for their tipis.

Making Things from Buffalo

The buffalo gave the people almost everything they needed to survive.

Parts and Uses
1. Hides and furs were used for robes, blankets, tipi covers, rugs, and shields.
2. Horns were used for spoons and headdresses.
3. Hair was used for rope.
4. Bones were used for arrowheads and sewing needles.
5. Meat and bones were eaten.
6. Tails were used as flyswatters.
7. Sinews were used for thread and twine.
8. Tongues were made into brushes.

CULTURE/CUSTOMS	
SHELTER	
FOOD	
SKILLS	

UTE

Utah is named after the Ute Indians. The name comes from a word the Spanish used when they met the Ute. The Ute called themselves by a different name—Nooch.

The Ute moved with the seasons. In the summer, they lived in tipis in the cool mountains. They hunted animals and fished in the lakes. They gathered berries, nuts, seeds, and plants. They made a kind of granola bar by mixing seeds and berries with animal fat and dried meat.

When winter came, they traveled to the warmer valleys and deserts. They made shelters out of brush, grass, and willows. A family might build several brush shelters in one year. They left them behind as they moved on. Each group went to the same areas year after year.

In warm weather, Ute men wore breechcloths. Women wore skirts made of shredded bark or leather. They wove reeds into strong sandals. In winter, women wore long dresses and leggings made of buffalo skins. Men wore shirts and leggings. Both men and women wore moccasins.

Buffalo were just as important to the Ute as they were to the Shoshone. Ute hunted buffalo, antelope, deer, and other animals. They hunted with bows and arrows, spears, clubs, and knives.

Skilled Horsemen and Basket-Makers

The Ute used horses to hunt, travel, and carry heavy loads. They were the first tribe in Utah to get horses. They got them by trading with the Spanish. The Ute became very skilled horsemen.

Pagre, Ute.

Ute women were often leaders among their people. One explorer said a Ute woman named Chipeta "exerts great influence and is much revered [looked up to with respect]." Women also made beautiful baskets and were known for their skill at tanning animal skins to make things like moccasins.

CULTURE/CUSTOMS

SHELTER

FOOD

SKILLS

GOSHUTE

The Goshute referred to themselves as Kuttuhsippeh. It meant "People of the Dry Earth." They lived in the hot, dry Great Salt Lake Desert.

The Goshute did not settle in one place and raise their food. They traveled the desert and nearby mountains searching for plants and animals to eat. There were a few small creeks where they could catch fish and water birds.

Finding Food in the Desert

The Goshute had an amazing knowledge of where to find food in the desert. In the spring, they ate the new green plants as greens. In the summer, they collected seeds and fruits in the valleys and flatlands. By the end of summer, roots and tubers were ready to eat. In the fall they moved to the mountains to harvest pine nuts. These are delicious nuts inside the cones of pinyon pine trees. They stored what they could for the winter.

Plant Experts

The Goshute could not have lived without plants. They knew that rabbitbrush stems made good arrows. The leaves helped treat colds and fevers. Yucca roots were crushed and eaten raw or roasted. The wood from a willow could be chewed to stop pain.

Plants and animals also provided clothing. In the hot summer, the people did not need to wear many clothes. Men wore a breechcloth. Women wore aprons or grass skirts. They used twigs to make sun shades for their heads. In the winter, the families had rabbit-skin blankets to help keep them warm. Goshute and Paiute built wickiups for shade and places to sleep.

CULTURE/CUSTOMS	
SHELTER	
FOOD	
SKILLS	

PAIUTE

The Paiute called themselves Nuwuvi. They moved about to find food and shelter. In the winter, the bands traveled to the winter deserts and valleys. In the summer, they lived in the cool mountains.

The Paiute made wickiups out of branches, juniper bark, and rushes. Later, they began to use canvas or animal skins. A family might build several wickiups. They might build one where they gathered seeds in July and another for gathering wild berries in the fall. They might build one at their fishing camp in the winter and another in a pine forest.

Adapting to the Desert
Some of the Paiute farmed. They used water from the Virgin River to irrigate corn, squash, beans, sunflowers, wheat, and melons.

Others lived near springs. They adapted to a desert environment. They hunted rabbits, deer, and mountain sheep. They gathered seeds, roots, berries, and nuts.

Paiute knew which plants were poisonous and which were good to eat. They knew which roots and bulbs to dig in the spring and which seeds and berries ripened in summer. Like other Indians, Paiute also used plants for medicine.

In the summer, men wore breechcloths, and women wore skirts. Women also wore aprons made from plant fibers and sometimes sandals. In the winter, everyone wore shirts and moccasins. They used blankets made of soft rabbit skins.

Cradleboards
Paiute were known for the cradleboards they made. Cradleboards were used to carry babies. A mother put her baby in the cradleboard and wore it on her back. When she stopped to work or rest, she might lean the cradleboard against a log or sturdy tree.

CULTURE/CUSTOMS	
SHELTER	
FOOD	
SKILLS	

NAVAJO

The Navajo called themselves Diné. They lived in one area for most of their lives. The tribe was divided into family clans. In a clan were fathers, mothers, children, grandparents, aunts, uncles, and cousins.

The Navajo lived in a dry region. Some clans irrigated and farmed. Corn was particularly important. Changing Woman (nature) gave instructions about how it should be raised and used. The Navajo also hunted a little. They used horses to hunt and carry loads.

Navajo used the wool from their sheep to make yarn. They dyed the yarn with colors from plants and berries. Then they wove the yarn into beautiful rugs, blankets, and cloth.

The Navajo also began to make jewelry using silver, coral, and turquoise.

Hogans

A Navajo family built a hogan to live in. It was meant to be filled with happiness. While the people were building it, they sang songs. The hogan stood for their spiritual connection to the Earth. Its door always faced east to meet the rising sun.

The people placed their hogans far apart from each other, not in villages. Today, most Navajo live in modern homes, but many still build hogans. They use them for family ceremonies.

Navajo Weavers

Sheepherders and Weavers

The Navajo raised sheep and goats. They got these animals by trading with the Spanish. They built wooden corrals for the animals. They became great sheepherders.

CULTURE/CUSTOMS	
SHELTER	
FOOD	
SKILLS	

FIVE HISTORIC TRIBES BRAIN TEASER

Now that you have learned about the Five Historic Tribes, see if you can answer the below questions without looking back at the reading material on the previous pages.

1. The Shoshone where known for their?

_____

2. This tribe had an amazing knowledge of where to find food in the desert.

_____

3. A Navajo family lived in this.

_____

4. This tribe's women were often leaders among their people.

_____

5. This tribe made wickiups out of branches, juniper bark, and rushes.

_____

6. This tribe farmed corn and raised sheep.

_____

7. Who called themselves Nimi?

_____

8. The Ute were the first tribe in Utah to get these animals.

_____

9. The Paiute used these to carry their babies.

_____

10. The Goshute used rabbitbrush stems to make what?

_____

FIELD TRIP: NATURAL HISTORY MUSEUM OF UTAH

The Natural History Museum of Utah is located at the Rio Tinto Center on the University of Utah campus. It is the perfect place to go explore and learn about everything from the sky to rocks to dinosaurs to Native Americans.

Plan a visit with your family and see the regular exhibits as well as the special events. While you are there, be sure to pay special attention to the First Peoples and the Native Voices exhibits.

What were some of the most memorable things you saw at the museum? What caught your attention for these items?

1. _____

_____

2. _____

_____

3. _____

_____

4. _____

_____

5. _____

_____

HOME, SWEET HOME

The Ute and Shoshone made and lived in tipis. Although the tipis are nothing like what we live in today, they did many of the same things in the tipi that we do in our homes. Read about the tipis to learn more about what is similar to your home today and what is different. Write your findings in the chart.

The Tipi

Tipis were perfect for people on the move. They were easy to take down, move, and put up again. The Ute and Shoshone made tipis.

Women usually had the job of making and caring for the tipis. They made a frame from wooden poles. They tied the tops of the poles together. Then they spread out the bottoms of the poles to form a cone shape. After that, they stretched animal hides they had sewn together over the poles.

People had fires inside the tipi for cooking, warmth, and light. They left the hides open at the top so smoke from the fire could come out. Inside they hung clothing, medicine bags, and shields. Often they decorated the outside of the tipi with designs and drawings of birds and animals. Some were decorated to tell the story of the tribe.

When people were ready to move, they packed up the tipi. They used its poles to make a travois. This was a carrier that the horses pulled along behind them.

READING & WRITING

What it was like inside a tipi.

_____

_____

_____

_____

_____

_____

_____

Things that are similar between tipis and my home.

_____

_____

_____

_____

_____

_____

_____

What it is like inside my home.

_____

_____

_____

_____

_____

_____

_____

LEGENDS

American Indian groups told legends as a way of explaining how something came to be. There is a legend to tell why the owl stays up late and how the land was created. Legends are fun because they include elements from nature and have an interesting way of explaining uninteresting things. There are many legends online and in books. The book, *Spider Spins a Story: Fourteen Legends from Native America*, by Jill Max was written for kids and is a great read.

Read this legend, "Why the Year Has 12 Months" to see if you can identify the elements of nature.

Why the Year Has 12 Months

It is winter, and you are tired of being inside. Your grandmother puts a few more sticks on the fire. She tells you and your brothers and sisters to come and sit around the fire. She begins to tell you a story. You listen closely. Someday you will tell this story to your own children.

Coyote and a large bird with 12 feathers in its tail were having an argument. They could not agree on how many months there should be in the year. Coyote said there should be as many months as there were hairs in his coat. The large bird, which was probably an eagle, said there should be as many months in the year as there were feathers in his tail.

After much talking, the bird ended it. He said there would be as many months in the year as there were feathers in his tail unless Coyote could catch him. Then the bird flew away. Because Coyote could not fly, he could not catch the bird. That is why there have been, to this day, 12 months in the year.

—adapted from a Goshute legend told by William Palmer in *Why the North Star Stands Still and Other Indian Legends.*

What elements of nature are in the legend?

_____

_____

_____

Now it's your turn to write a legend! Legends are short because they were passed down from person to person before people could read or write. Keep yours short enough to retell without having to read it.

What will you explain? (Examples: Why the sky is blue, why the night is dark, how babies learn to walk)

_____

What elements of nature will you use?

_____

Beginning: Introduce your characters and the problem.

_____

_____

_____

Middle: Tell the steps taken to solve the problem.

_____

_____

_____

End: Tell what the end result is. Include a statement like "And that's why . . ."

_____

_____

_____

UTAH'S MOUNTAIN MEN

The next few pages contain details about Utah's mountain men. These were well-known men who trapped in, traveled through, and lived in Utah's mountains. As you read, highlight a few important details about each mountain man. It should be just a few words or phrases that you think make him important to remember.

Etienne Provost

Etienne Provost was born in Canada. He worked as a trapper in Missouri and New Mexico before traveling to Utah. He may have been the first white person to see the Great Salt Lake.

Provost set up trading posts next to the Great Salt Lake and Utah Lake. He was very skilled at living outdoors. His friends called him "the man of the mountains." Can you guess what city and river are named for Provost?

Provost was involved in a clash with the Shoshone. A group of mountain men had stolen horses and fur from the Shoshone and killed one of their men. To strike back, a group of Shoshone attacked Provost. He and a few of his men escaped. The rest were killed.

Jim Bridger

Jim Bridger had not gone to school much, but he was a great storyteller. Besides English, he spoke French, Spanish, and several Indian languages.

Bridger came to Utah when he was about 20. His group entered Cache Valley and camped on the Bear River. His men tried to guess where the river ended. Bridger wanted to find out. He followed the river in a boat until it flowed into a large body of water. He tasted the water and found it very salty. He thought he might have reached the Pacific Ocean. Some historians think Bridger (not Provost) was the first white man to see the Great Salt Lake.

Bridger and others started the Rocky Mountain Fur Company. He also built a fort in Wyoming where travelers could stop and rest. At Fort Bridger, travelers could trade for blankets, sugar, gunpowder, and other supplies.

Peter Skene Ogden

Peter Skene Ogden was born in Canada. He became a fur trapper there. Then the Hudson's Bay Company hired him. His job was to lead men throughout the West in search of beaver. On his second trip to Utah, he explored the Great Salt Lake and the area that is now named for him. He called Ogden Valley a "hole" because mountains completely surrounded it.

In his journal, Ogden wrote that the land was swarming with huge black crickets. The air was filled with seagulls. It was one of the earliest written accounts of the region. Both Ogden City and the Ogden River are named after Peter Skene Ogden.

Louis Vasquez

Louis Vasquez was from Missouri. He came to Utah in search of beavers. He and three other trappers paddled their boats all the way around the Great Salt Lake. Like others, they thought it might be part of the ocean. They wanted to find out. They also wanted to find streams that flowed into the lake so they could trap beavers. It took them about a month to go around the entire lake. When they found there were no rivers leaving the lake, they knew it was a "Great Inland Sea."

After trapping, Vasquez became a businessman. He and his friend Jim Bridger build Fort Bridger on the Green River. Before that, he and a friend had built Fort Vasquez in Colorado. Today, it is a museum about the fur trade.

Vasquez married a woman named Narcissa Ashcraft. The two of them opened a store in Salt Lake City. They sold supplies that travelers to California needed.

James Beckwourth

James Beckwourth was born a slave in Virginia. Beckwourth's father was white, and his mother was his father's black slave. When James was a teenager, he moved with his family to Missouri.

Beckwourth first worked as a blacksmith. In 1822, he went west to be a trapper. He spent a lot of time in the Salt Lake and Cache valleys. Then a tribe of Crow Indians captured him. They adopted him. He lived with them for eight or nine years. He married a Crow woman and became a chief. For the rest of his life, he often dressed like the Crow.

After Beckwourth left the Crow, he worked at many different jobs. He was a miner, army scout, rancher, and businessman. He was also an explorer. He discovered a pass in the high Sierra Nevada. Beckwourth Pass is the lowest place to cross the mountains between California and Nevada. He blazed a trail through the mountains called Beckwourth Trail. People traveling to California soon began to use this route across the mountains.

Jedediah Smith

The life of a fur trapper was dangerous. When Jedediah Smith was in South Dakota, a grizzly bear attacked him. It ripped one of his ears and part of his scalp almost all the way off. He had to ask one of his friends, James Clyman, to sew his ear on again.

Smith led a group through southwestern Utah and Nevada. They trudged across the Mojave Desert in the burning sun. They almost died because they could not find enough food or water. At last, they wandered into a Spanish mission in California. Later, they crossed the Sierra Nevada, rode their horses across Nevada, and returned to Utah. The men made their way to Bear Lake. When they arrived at the rendezvous, there was much rejoicing. Smith's friends had thought he was dead!

Smith was probably the first trapper to go all the way from St. Louis to the California coast. He was the first to travel across Utah's length and width. He clearly showed that no rivers flowed from the Great Salt Lake into the Pacific Ocean. He also found South Pass, which made the route through the Wyoming mountains shorter.

Now, use the information that you highlighted to write one or two sentences that tell about each mountain man. Then draw either a

ETIENNE PROVOST

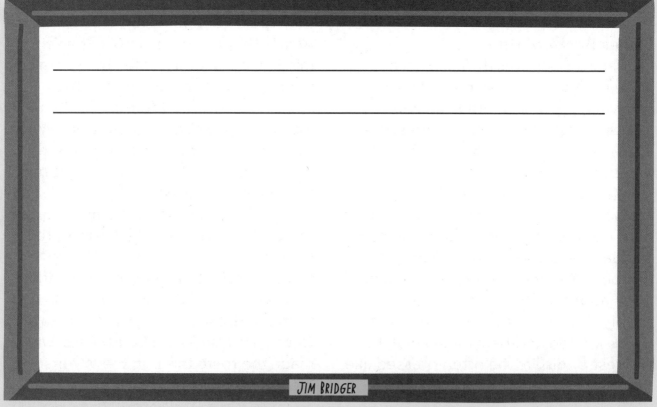

JIM BRIDGER

picture of them doing something you read about them doing, a place they visited, or anything related to what you know about them.

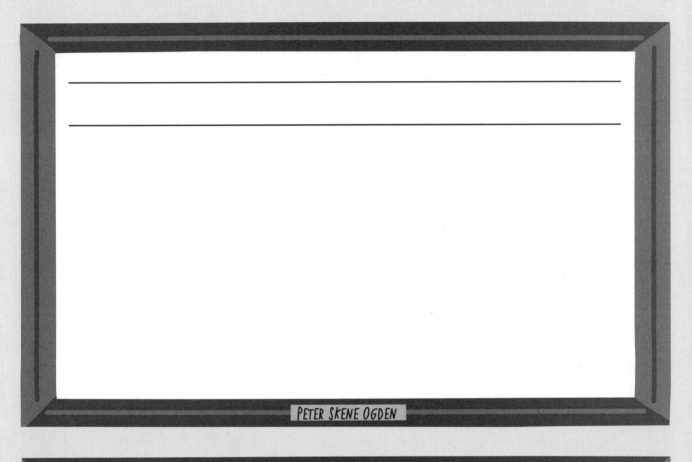

PETER SKENE OGDEN

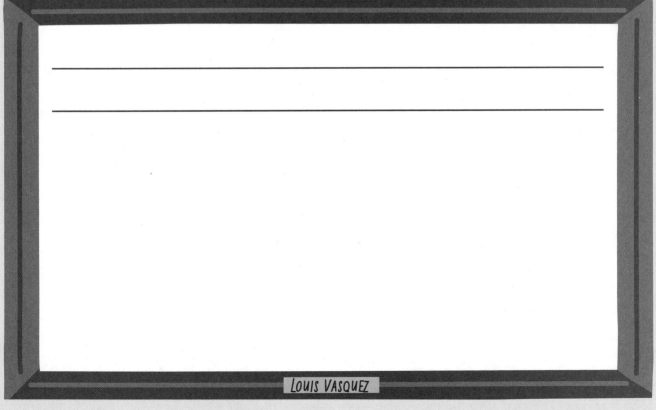

LOUIS VASQUEZ

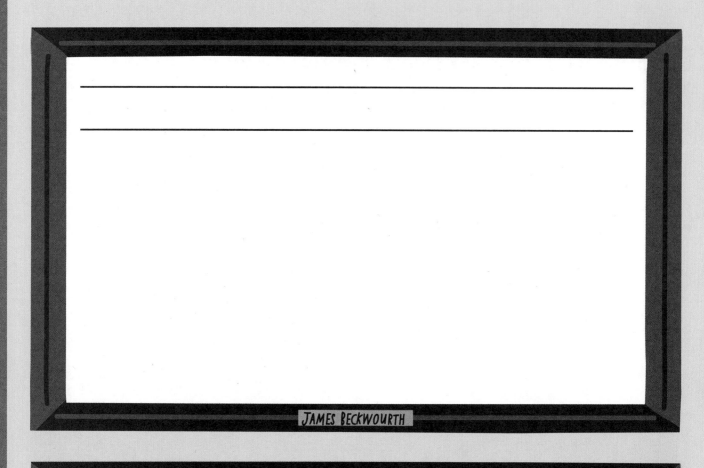

JAMES BECKWOURTH

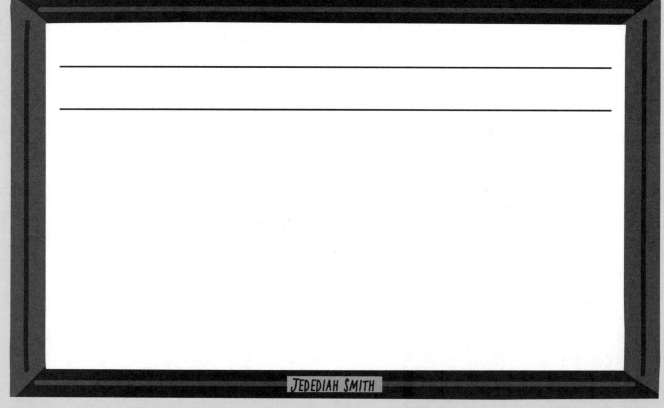

JEDEDIAH SMITH

MOUNTAIN MAN SCRAMBLE

Unscramble each of the clue words. Take the letters that appear in circled boxes and unscramble them to answer the question, what were the mountain men famous for?

NIEENET ROSPOVT

☐ ☐ ☐ ☐ ◯ ☐ ☐   ☐ ◯ ◯ ◯ ☐ ◯ ◯

MIJ RDRIEGB

☐ ◯ ☐   ☐ ☐ ☐ ☐ ◯ ◯ ◯

EPTER SEKNE GEDNO

☐ ☐ ◯ ☐   ☐ ◯ ☐ ◯ ☐   ◯ ☐ ◯ ☐ ☐

IUSOL SUAVEZQ

◯ ◯ ☐ ☐ ☐   ☐ ☐ ◯ ☐ ◯ ◯ ◯

SEJAM KOEWUBCTHR

☐ ◯ ☐ ☐ ◯   ☐ ☐ ☐ ☐ ◯ ☐ ☐ ☐ ☐ ◯

JADEDHEI MSHIT

☐ ☐ ☐ ☐ ☐ ◯ ☐ ☐   ☐ ◯ ☐ ◯ ☐ ◯

☐ ☐ ☐ ☐ ☐ ☐ ☐   ☐ F F ☐   ☐ ☐ ☐ ☐ ☐

☐ ☐ ☐ ☐ L ☐   ☐ ☐

☐ ☐ ☐ ☐ ☐ ☐ ☐ ☐ ☐ ☐ ☐

FIELD TRIP: FORT BUENAVENTURA STATE PARK

To see what it was like to live in the time of the mountain men and fur trappers, plan a visit to Fort Buenaventura State Park on the Weber River near downtown Ogden. You can camp there and canoe and even visit a trading post.

Every Easter weekend, the park hosts a rendezvous that is a great reenactment of the rendezvous the mountain men used to have. You can watch people practice skills such as shooting guns and throwing knives. Or, maybe you can barter for some fur pelts.

Draw a picture of yourself dressed up as a mountain man or a mountain woman. What kind of survival skills do you have?

MOUNTAIN MAN LIMERICK

Limericks are fun poems that have five lines. Lines 1, 2, and 5 rhyme and are long lines. And lines 3 and 4 rhyme and are short lines. Write a limerick about a specific mountain man you read about in the previous pages.

Here is an example:
There once was an explorer named Bridger.
He went to find the end of Bear River.
He found the Salt Lake.
Fort Bridger he did make,
And he traded furs with great vigor!

1. _____

_____

_____

2. _____

_____

_____

3. _____

_____

4. _____

_____

5. _____

_____

PACKING LIST

What would you pack if you were leaving for months to go explore an unknown land? Read about important government explorations planned by the U.S. government. The men were sent to learn more about Utah and the rest of the Great Basin region. After reading, decide what you would pack if you were traveling with John C. Fremont or Major John Wesley Powell.

Government Explorers

As the fur trade ended, the U.S. government sent explorers out west. Their job was to map the land. The government hoped to make it U.S. territory someday.

John C. Fremont

John C. Fremont led five expeditions to the West. He had help from former mountain men. His team also included

an African American named Jacob Dodson. The men searched for a water route from the Great Salt Lake to California. They named Pilot Peak, after it helped guide them through the salt flats.

Fremont's crew explored the Great Salt Lake and the area around it. They traveled the Bear River. They explored the area around St. George and Santa Clara.

Fremont is known as the one who finally found a way west from the Salt Lake Valley to California. His work added

to what people knew about the West. Every day, he took the temperature of the air. He measured elevation and collected soil samples. He wrote about the Indian people he met and the plants and animals. He also made important maps. His wife, Jessie, helped him publish his reports. Later she wrote to him, "All your campfires have become cities."

In time, Fremont moved to California. He became a U.S. senator (after California became a part of the United States). He even ran for president of the United States. He was not elected.

Later Government Explorers

The government sent other men to explore and map Utah. They included Captain Howard Stansbury, John W. Gunnison, and Major John Wesley Powell.

Powell explored the unmapped parts of the Colorado and Green rivers. In wooden boats, he and his men rode the churning rapids and chutes. Powell was the first man to travel all the way down the two rivers through the Grand Canyon. He also worked for laws that would save and protect the land and its amazing waters.

The maps these explorers made were more accurate than earlier maps. Their reports taught the rest of the country more about the West.

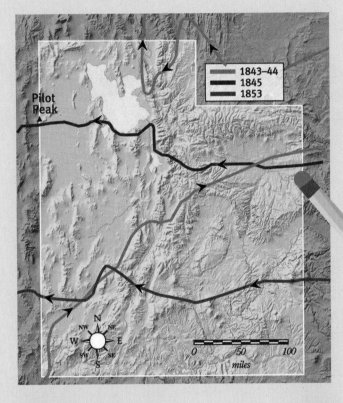

Pilot Peak

1843–44
1845
1853

N
NW   NE
W   E
SW   SE
S

0   50   100
miles

FOOD ITEMS:
_____
_____
_____

TOOLS:
_____
_____
_____

CLOTHING ITEMS:
_____
_____
_____
_____

ITEMS FOR PROTECTION:
_____
_____
_____

BOOKS, MAPS, AND WRITING MATERIALS:
_____
_____
_____
_____

ANYTHING ELSE:
_____
_____
_____

ITEMS USED TO TRAVEL WITH:
_____
_____
_____

AND DON'T FORGET ... SOMETHING TO CARRY ALL OF THIS:
_____
_____

A DAY IN THE LIFE OF AN EXPLORER

Imagine that you were a member of the group of government explorers sent to explore Utah and the surrounding area in the 1840s and 1850s. Where in Utah did you travel? What did you see? What did Utah look like at that time? Write a journal entry from the

_____

_____

_____

_____

_____

_____

_____

_____

_____

_____

_____

_____

perspective of an explorer. Include details about your exploration that day. What might people want to hear about when you return to the big cities on the east coast? Explorers were expected to be very detailed in their reports of newly explored places.

_____

_____

_____

_____

_____

_____

_____

_____

_____

_____

_____

_____

WORTH THE RISK?

Passing through the Great Basin

People in the East began hearing about the land out west. They talked to people who had been there. They read letters, news articles, and reports from explorers.

In the 1840s, many people began moving west. They wanted to settle in California and Oregon Country. Oregon Country included the land that is now Washington, Oregon, and parts of Montana and Idaho. It was a huge region.

On their way to California and Oregon, some people passed through the land we call Utah. But they did not stay. They wanted a milder climate and fertile land to farm. Utah's land and climate seemed too harsh and dry to them.

Making the Journey

The main trail west was the Oregon Trail. At one point, the trail split. Some travelers went to Oregon Country and others to California. The path to California became known as the California Trail.

Travelers carried their belongings in wooden wagons pulled by oxen or mules. One group followed another, making a long line called a wagon train. The pioneers' horses and cattle walked behind.

The group moved very slowly, often just 12 miles a day. (Today, you can travel 12 miles in 12 minutes by car!) The trail followed rivers most of the way. Travelers had to cross the flat plains and then go through the steep Rocky Mountains.

By the time Mormon pioneers came to Utah to make it their home, many people had been here. A lot of people knew about Utah. So far though, most people were just passing through.

Early Routes through the Great Basin

What do you think? Was it worth the risks to travel west on the Oregon or California Trails? Use information from what you just read to support your answer. Give at least three reasons.

_____

_____

_____

_____

_____

_____

_____

_____

_____

_____

_____

_____

_____

_____

_____

_____

CAMPFIRES

John C. Fremont led multiple expeditions all over what is now the western United States. The reports he brought back about the land made many people eager to move west. Fremont's wife, Jessie Benton Fremont, said to her husband, "All your campfires have become cities."

What do you think she meant by this statement?

_____

_____

_____

_____

_____

Who might have liked and disliked the changes Fremont's wife was referring to? Why?

_____

_____

_____

_____

_____

_____

"THEIR FACES TOWARD ZION"

The Mormons

Pioneers continued to pass through the dry Utah region. They did not try to stay and settle here. Then in 1847, a group of people moved to Utah. After American Indians, they were the next people who wanted Utah to be their home. They were the Mormons.

"Mormon" was a nickname for people who belonged to a new church. They were called Mormons because they believed in a book called *The Book of Mormon.* The church's real name was The Church of Jesus Christ of Latter-Day Saints (or LDS for short).

Choosing Utah

The Mormons decided to move far away from other people. They thought about many places—California, Canada, and Texas. The place they finally chose was Utah. (The land we call Utah was still not a part of the United States. It was part of Mexico at this time.)

Mormons chose Utah because it was isolated. It was a long way from other cities. They hoped they would be left alone and would not have trouble with their neighbors. They hoped other pioneers would continue to pass it by.

These Mormons are often referred to as pioneers. However, a pioneer is anyone who is the first to do something. Describe a time when you were a pioneer. Include details about the challenge and how it turned out in the end.

_____

_____

_____

_____

_____

_____

FIELD TRIP: THIS IS THE PLACE HERITAGE PARK

This Is the Place Heritage Park is a step back in time. You can pretend to be in the old West for a day and visit a village from the pioneer days or tour a Native American community. You can ride ponies and trains, make friends with farm animals, or even pan for gold. There are also blacksmith, tinsmith, and saddle maker shops to go along with a mercantile store and an old hotel.

After your field trip to This is the Place Heritage Park, write down some thoughts about pioneer life. What was it like? Would you have liked to live then? Why or why not?

_____

_____

_____

_____

_____

_____

_____

_____

_____

_____

Draw yourself as a pioneer and then draw three of your favorite activities from the day.

The Mormon Trail

The Mormons sent an "advance company" to the Salt Lake Valley. Its job was to go first and prepare the way for others. A few months later, more Mormon pioneers came. By the time winter began, there were nearly 2,000 people there. Every year after that, thousands more came. By the time the railroad came to Utah, more than 80,000 people had *migrated* here.

Imagine what it was like to travel in a wagon train! The most common wagons were covered wagons. They were ordinary farm wagons with heavy, sturdy wheels. They had canvas covers to protect their loads. From a distance, they looked like small ships swaying across the wide plains. Their white canvas tops ballooned and whipped in the wind.

Horses and oxen pulled the wagons. Very small children rode in them. Mostly though, the people walked beside them. Later, some pioneers had to pull handcarts across the plains.

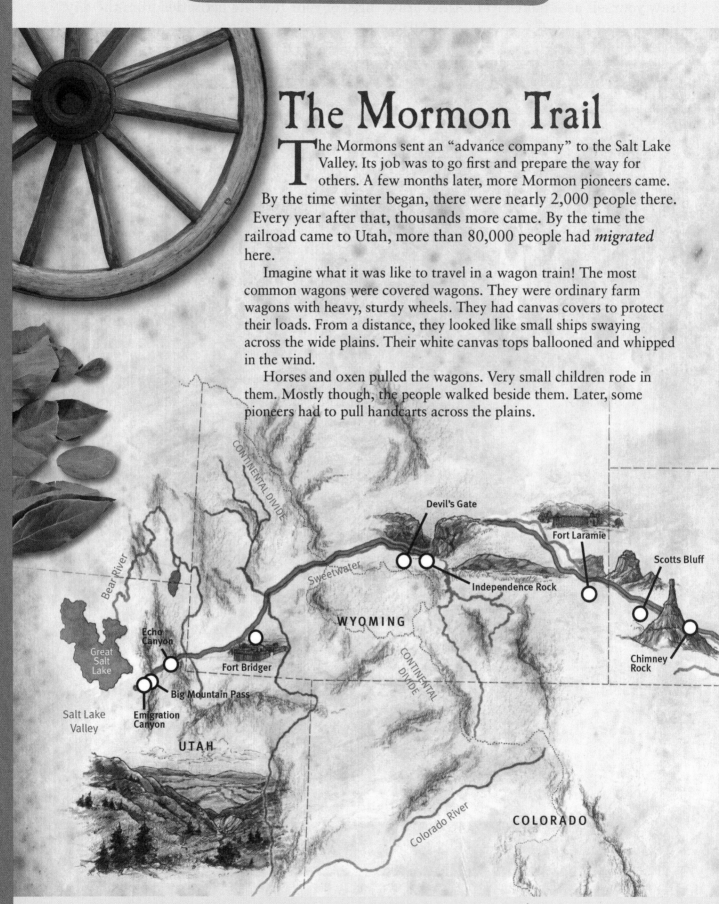

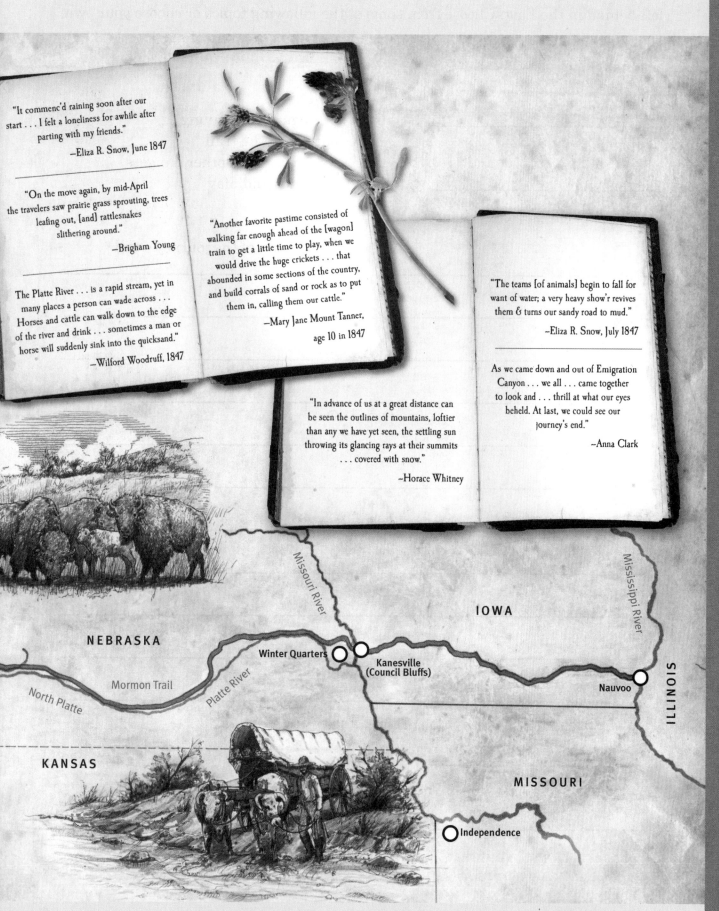

"It commenc'd raining soon after our start . . . I felt a loneliness for awhile after parting with my friends."

—Eliza R. Snow, June 1847

"On the move again, by mid-April the travelers saw prairie grass sprouting, trees leafing out, [and] rattlesnakes slithering around."

—Brigham Young

The Platte River . . . is a rapid stream, yet in many places a person can wade across . . . Horses and cattle can walk down to the edge of the river and drink . . . sometimes a man or horse will suddenly sink into the quicksand."

—Wilford Woodruff, 1847

"Another favorite pastime consisted of walking far enough ahead of the [wagon] train to get a little time to play, when we would drive the huge crickets . . . that abounded in some sections of the country, and build corrals of sand or rock as to put them in, calling them our cattle."

—Mary Jane Mount Tanner, age 10 in 1847

"In advance of us at a great distance can be seen the outlines of mountains, loftier than any we have yet seen, the settling sun throwing its glancing rays at their summits . . . covered with snow."

—Horace Whitney

"The teams [of animals] begin to fall for want of water; a very heavy show'r revives them & turns our sandy road to mud."

—Eliza R. Snow, July 1847

As we came down and out of Emigration Canyon . . . we all . . . came together to look and . . . thrill at what our eyes beheld. At last, we could see our journey's end."

—Anna Clark

NEBRASKA

IOWA

Missouri River

Winter Quarters

Kanesville (Council Bluffs)

Mormon Trail

Platte River

North Platte

Mississippi River

Nauvoo

ILLINOIS

KANSAS

MISSOURI

Independence

Imagine you were a pioneer on the Mormon Trail. Write a letter to your friends you left behind in the East. Choose from some of the following topics or choose your own:

_____
(DATE)

_____,
(GREETING)

TOPICS
feelings about leaving
nature on the trail
waterways and other dangers
pastimes and play
weather
terrain
description of the journey's end

_____

_____

_____

_____

_____

_____

_____

_____

_____

_____

_____,
(CLOSING)

_____
(SIGNATURE)

SETTLERS AND INDIANS

As more and more settlers came to Utah, Indians began to be pushed off of their lands. Some settlers and Indians were able to live peacefully together. Other times, Indians and settlers fought with one another over the land. In the end, most Indians were forced into signing agreements with the U.S. government that they would give up their land in exchange for small pieces of land set aside for the Indians called reservations.

Imagine you are an Indian leader. You are faced with a difficult decision. If you keep fighting, more of your people will die. If you agree to peace, you will be moved to a reservation. The reservation is not as good for your people as the land you are fighting for. What would you do?

Indian Farms and Reservations, 2010

SCIENCE

IT'S NATURAL!

Utah has many useful natural resources. The resource map shows some of them and where in our state they are found. Compare this map to the map of Utah's cities and towns. Use the information to help you answer the questions on page 190.

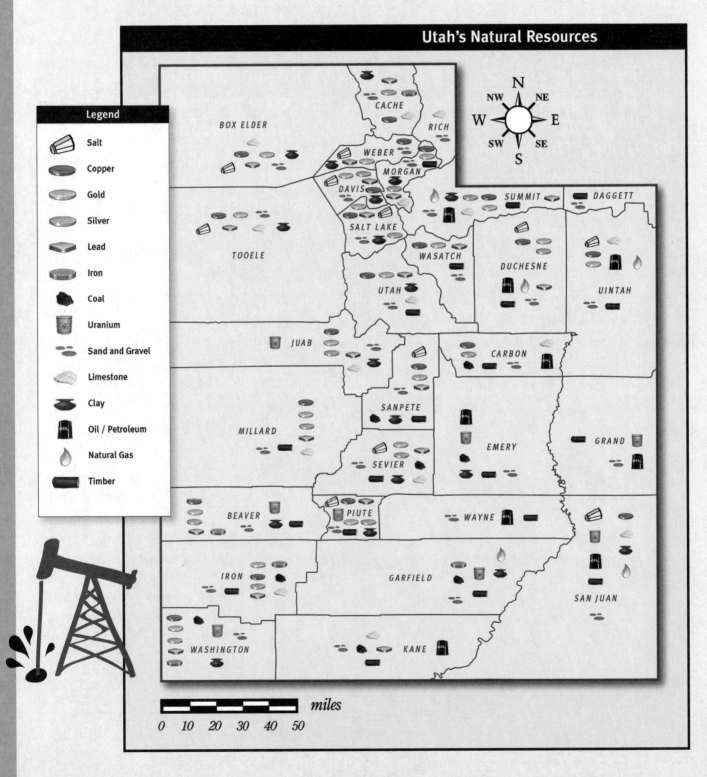

Utah's Natural Resources

Legend

- Salt
- Copper
- Gold
- Silver
- Lead
- Iron
- Coal
- Uranium
- Sand and Gravel
- Limestone
- Clay
- Oil / Petroleum
- Natural Gas
- Timber

miles
0   10   20   30   40   50

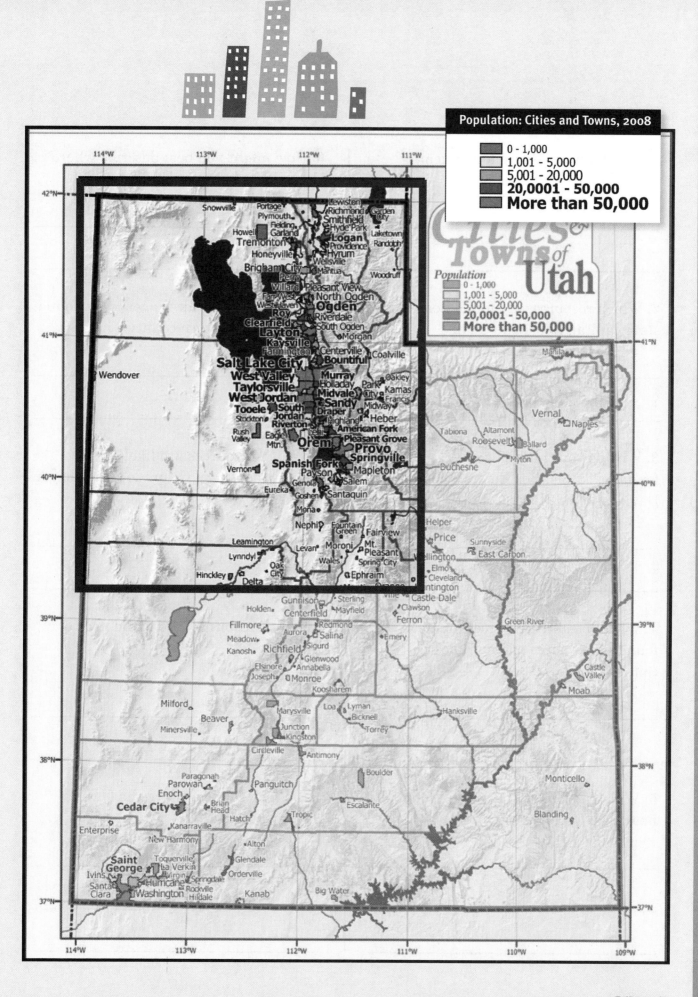

Cities & Towns of Utah

Population: Cities and Towns, 2008
- 0 - 1,000
- 1,001 - 5,000
- 5,001 - 20,000
- **20,0001 - 50,000**
- **More than 50,000**

Population
- 0 - 1,000
- 1,001 - 5,000
- 5,001 - 20,000
- 20,0001 - 50,000
- More than 50,000

1. Which resources are found near where you live?

_____

_____

2. Which resources are found near our state capital, Salt Lake City?

_____

_____

3. Why do you think salt is a resource found in Tooele, Box Elder, Weber, Davis, and Salt Lake Counties?

_____

_____

4. Which natural resources are not found in the three northernmost counties?

_____

_____

5. Which natural resources are found near Bear Lake?

_____

_____

6. How might you best describe where Uranium is found in Utah?

_____

_____

7. Why do you think timber is not found in all of the western counties in Utah?

_____

_____

8. Which resources are likely to be found in southern Colorado? How do you know?

_____

_____

9. Which resources are found near Blanding?

_____

_____

10. Which counties have the fewest natural resources?

_____

_____

UTAH'S NATURAL RESOURCES WORD SEARCH

Finding natural resources can often be difficult and time consuming. See if you can locate all of the words from the list in the below word search. Circle every word you find.

CLAY   COAL   COPPER   GOLD   IRON   LEAD   LIMESTONE

NATURAL GAS   OIL   PETROLEUM   SALT   SAND AND GRAVEL

SILVER   TIMBER   URANIUM

```
L V S P Z H Y M R N L J C F C V M L I C
P E D G V M V J E W G V N D O M L J A S
Z T V B H L U N F D K S P E P Q W W I K
Y C S A F T O G A Q Q E E U P U F L R M
I R O N R T F E R Q B N U E E T V N P L
C I E I S G L H S G L C B G R E R V A J
O M Y E X I D O G Y R K C G S K Q K K K
U E M B F N T N F H S U F B I A K K U P
N I C J Z A Q K A C G I E J S G L U A V
L I L T N C T K E D P E T R O L E U M I
C Z A Y L S S L T L N M G K V A O L O J
U E Y A U F N T T L C A O W X R T W H U
X R G B U D Y V J F A I S S R U L F C R
G T A B N Y H Y N X L S R A U T D D O S
V B B N C P H P Y S B D X K K A B N Q U
Y X P X I O W S S T V P X A W N L X S V
I B F Z M U A F C H D O A W P C I J I L
U S E O A O M L I K L R H P N V U J O W
J W P H R E B M I T O T X E Z Q M X Q G
B G N E W L I P H Z G K T A U I H V H K
```

WEATHER WIZARDS

Utah's weather can change from cold and snowy to warm and sunny in a matter of minutes. How different is the weather across our state? Record the weather patterns of your city over a ten-day period. Do the same for a Utah city far away from you. Compare your findings to learn just how crazy Utah's weather can be! Visit a local news station website or a national weather website, such as www.weather.com to find the information for the faraway city.

	YOUR CITY HIGH TEMPERATURE	YOUR CITY PRECIPITATION	COMPARISON CITY HIGH TEMPERATURE	COMPARISON CITY PRECIPITATION
Day 1				
Day 2				
Day 3				
Day 4				
Day 5				
Day 6				
Day 7				
Day 8				
Day 9				
Day 10				

Describe how your weather compares to that of the faraway city.

_____

_____

Why do you think your weather findings were similar/different?

_____

_____

Which city's weather do you prefer? Why?

_____

_____

CLOUD GAZING

Sometimes people see shapes in the clouds like animals or faces. Spend 30 minutes or more just lying on a blanket in the grass looking at the sky. Did you see any fun shapes in the clouds while you were gazing? Draw a picture of what you saw.

CLOUD YOUR VISION

The clouds can tell us a lot about the weather. There are three main types of clouds: stratus, cumulus, and cirrus. Read about the different types below. Then use the information to help Megan and Dan decide what to wear to school.

Stratus Clouds

Stratus clouds are the closest to the ground and seem to blanket the sky. At about 6,500 feet, they can produce rain, drizzle, snow, or mist.

Cumulus Clouds

Cumulus clouds are puffy and white. Often they are flat on the bottom and rise up like huge pieces of cotton. They form up to 20,000 feet above the ground. Cumulus clouds usually mean fair weather. But they sometimes grow very large and become thunderheads. As these clouds gather, they create thunder and lightning and produce rain and hail.

Cirrus Clouds

Cirrus clouds are thin, curly, wispy clouds. They form 25,000 to 40,000 feet above the ground. They are so high that the water droplets freeze into ice crystals. Cirrus clouds generally signal an incoming storm or a change in weather.

What kind of clouds Megan and Dan saw out the window this morning:	What you think the weather might be like today:	What kinds of clothes and shoes you think Megan and Dan should wear to school today:
GREY STRATUS CLOUDS BLANKET THE SKY.		
EVEN MORE AND DARKER STRATUS CLOUDS BLANKET THE SKY.		
THE SUN IS SHINING AND THERE ARE A FEW CIRRUS CLOUDS IN THE SKY.		
THE SUN IS SHINING AND WHITE CUMULUS CLOUDS ARE IN THE SKY.		
VERY LARGE GREY CUMULUS CLOUDS ARE IN THE SKY.		

THE LAKE EFFECT

Northern Utah gets lake-effect rain and snow. A lake effect is when a body of water gives the land around it a more moist and moderate climate. It does not get quite as hot or cold as the other places, but it often gets more rain and snow. Label the Lake Effect diagram using the words from the word bank below.

CLOUDS FORM.

THE WARMED AIR RISES, TAKING MOISTURE WITH IT.

RAIN AND SNOW FALL OVER THE LAKE AND ON THE SHORE.

COLD AIR MOVES OVER WARM LAKE WATERS.

FIELD TRIP: THE GREAT SALT LAKE

Plan a day when you can go to see the Great Salt Lake. It doesn't matter which part of the lake you go to or what time of the year; you will still see something interesting.

Before you go, do some Internet research to learn about the lake. Look at a map to see where it is in relationship to where you live. How large is it? Does it always stay the same size? Where do lake-effect winter storms usually occur?

Write down three interesting facts about the lake.

1. _____

_____

2. _____

_____

3. _____

_____

What did you observe at the lake?

_____

_____

_____

_____

_____

_____

_____

UTAH'S THREE CLIMATES

A climate is the weather patterns found in a certain area. Most people think of Utah as a desert. However, Utah's climate changes as you move around the state.

Desert climates exist in areas with the least amounts of rain.

Steppe climates exist in dry areas where grasses and shrubs grow. Part of our state, the part where most of Utah's people live, is in the Great Basin. This is the part of our state with the steppe climate.

Highland (Mountain) climates exist in higher elevations with cooler temperatures. There is enough rain in these climates to support forests.

Is Utah mostly a desert, steppe, or mountain climate?

_____

About one-third of our state is which climate?

_____

Which climate is least common in Utah?

_____

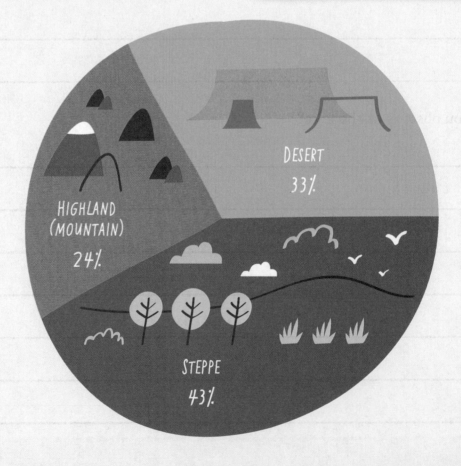

HIGHLAND (MOUNTAIN) 24%

DESERT 33%

STEPPE 43%

The Great Basin

The Great Basin is a region of the United States that includes most of Nevada, and parts of Utah, Oregon, Idaho, and California. It is an area of about 190,000 square miles that spans between the Sierra Nevada Mountains on its west side and the Wasatch Mountains on its east side. The Columbia Plateau is north of the basin with the Mojave Desert to the south. The Great Basin gets its name from its rivers and waterways that do not drain out to the oceans, but rather drain within the basin.

Climate Scrapbook

The plants, animals, and landforms of a region tell us about the climate. Different features can be found in Utah's three climates. Find pictures on the Internet to help illustrate each of these climates. Cut out the images and paste them below to make a climate scrapbook!

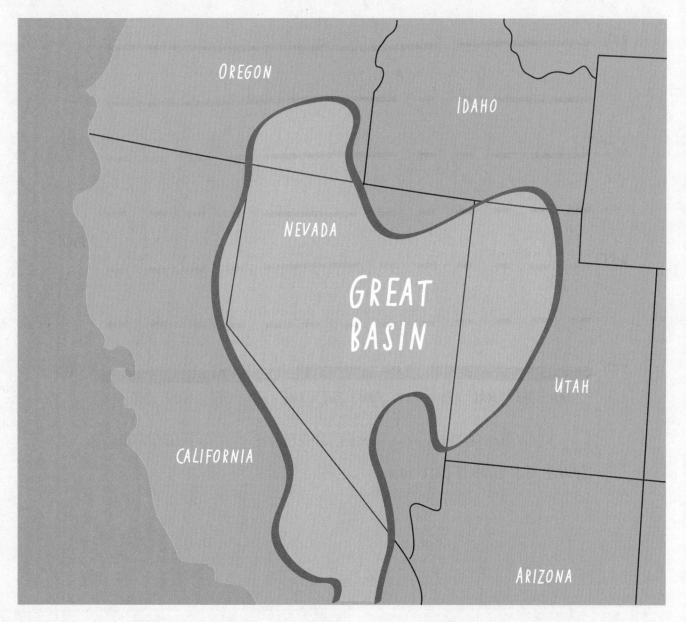

A CLIMO-WHAT?

A climograph is a graph that shows the average temperatures and precipitation of a place. This climograph shows data for Salt Lake City, Utah's capital city. Study the graph and answer the questions.

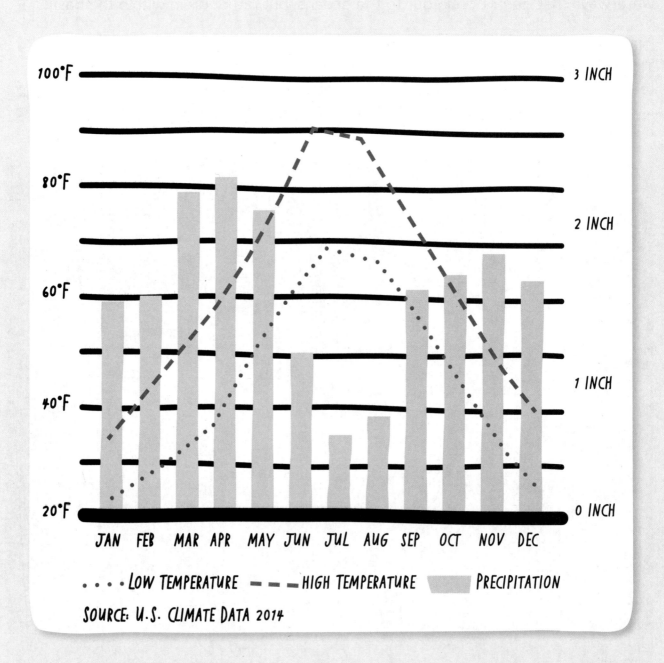

SOURCE: U.S. CLIMATE DATA 2014

1. Which color line represents the average high temperatures?

_____

2. Which color line represents the average low temperatures?

_____

3. Each line represents an increase of how many degrees?

_____

4. How are the amounts of precipitation represented?

_____

5. During which month(s) does Salt Lake City reach its highest temperatures?

_____

6. During which month(s) does Salt Lake City reach its lowest temperatures?

_____

7. Describe the pattern the high temperatures follow through the year.

_____

_____

8. Describe the pattern the low temperatures follow through the year.

_____

_____

9. Describe the pattern the precipitation follows through the year.

_____

_____

10. Do you think there is a relationship between the temperatures and the precipitation levels? Defend your answer with data from the climograph.

_____

_____

_____

WONDERFUL WATER

Utah is the second driest state in the nation. Water is a precious natural resource here! The amount and size of bodies of water nearby can affect how much precipitation (water that falls to the ground) an area gets. How? Understanding the water cycle will help you answer that question!

Read about the water cycle and label each step of the cycle on the diagram.

EVAPORATION: It all starts with heat from the sun. As the sun heats water, the water evaporates. That means it turns into vapor, or steam. The vapor rises into the air. Have you ever noticed a puddle that was there one day and gone the next? Where did the water go? It evaporated. Can you see the word vapor in evaporate?

CONDENSATION: When the water vapor in the air gets cold, it condenses (gets thicker) and turns back into liquid. You have seen this happen when you pour a glass of cold water on a hot day. Drops of water form on the outside of the glass. It also happens to the cool mirror in the bathroom when you take a hot shower.

As water condenses, clouds form. As more water condenses, the clouds get heavier.

PRECIPITATION: Pretty soon the air can no longer hold all that water. The water falls to the ground as rain, hail, sleet, or snow. This is called precipitation. The type of precipitation is based on the temperature.

COLLECTION: The falling water collects where it lands. It may fall in the rivers, lakes, and oceans. It may sink into the earth and become groundwater. Water that flows off the surface is called runoff. In time, it flows into the ocean or the Great Salt Lake. Then the cycle starts all over again.

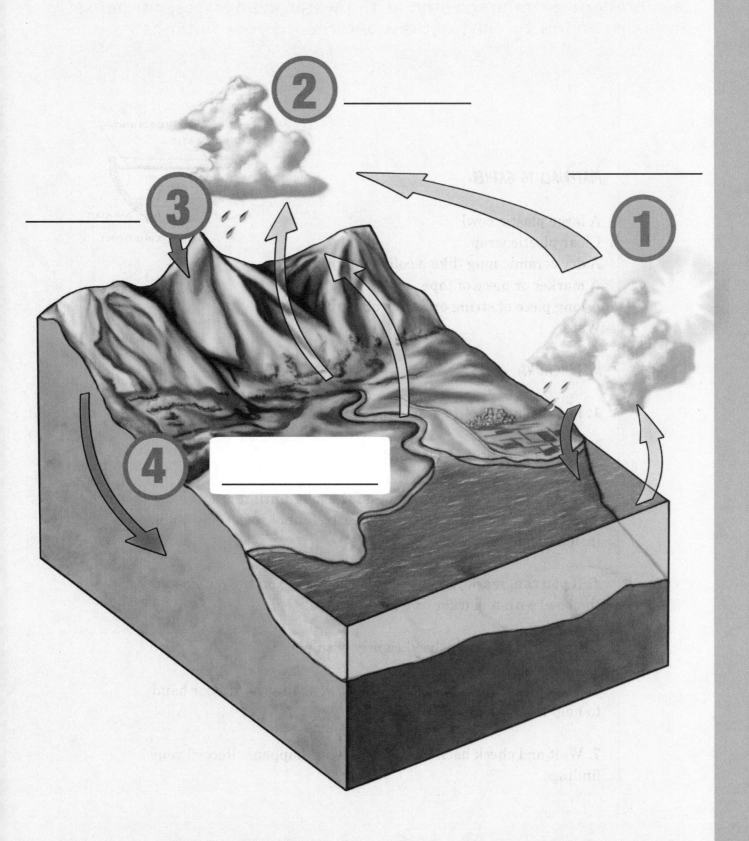

THE WATER CYCLE

Do you want to see the water cycle in action? You can create your own body of water and watch as the water evaporates, condenses, and falls. Follow the instructions and record your findings.

MATERIALS TO GATHER:

A large plastic bowl
Clear plastic wrap
A dry ceramic mug (like a coffee mug)
A marker or piece of tape
A long piece of string or large rubber band
Water

INSTRUCTIONS:

1. Put the large bowl outside in a sunny place.

2. Put the mug inside the bowl.

3. Add water into the bowl around the mug until it reaches up about $2/3$ the height of the mug. Be careful not to get any water inside the mug.

4. If you can, mark the beginning water level on the outside of the bowl with a marker or a piece of tape.

5. Cover the top of the bowl tightly with plastic wrap.

6. Either tie the string around the bowl or use the rubber band to help keep the plastic wrap on tight.

7. Wait and check back often to see what happens. Record your findings.

TIME Record the time you look at the bowl.	FINDINGS Record what you see.	CONCLUSIONS Record why you think things look like they do at this time.
START TIME:		
30 MINUTES LATER:		
ONE HOUR LATER:		
TWO HOURS LATER:		
THREE HOURS LATER:		
THE FOLLOWING DAY:		

THREE REGIONS, THREE ENVIRONMENTS

Because Utah has three distinct land regions, that means it has three distinct environments. Read about Utah's three environments and then write forest, desert, or wetlands on the line next to the animals or plants to show where they live.

Forests

In the cool forests, you can smell the leaves and the trees. You can hear woodpeckers drilling into tree trunks. A hummingbird whizzes by. Listen to the squirrels chattering! A deer raises its head, munching a leaf. Fish rise to the surface of a cold lake.

Forests are found in the mountains of Utah. On the lower slopes, there are oak, sagebrush, and aspen trees. These trees lose their leaves in the fall. Higher up, there are pine, spruce, hemlock, and fir trees. The higher trees keep their needles all year round.

Deserts

The flat deserts are so hot and dry. Plants and animals have adapted to the harsh land. That means they have changed their ways in order to survive there. The desert tortoise moves slowly across the sand. Prairie dogs dig holes under the ground, where it is cooler. Lizards, snakes, and insects hide between rocks and under plants.

Animals live in the cold deserts as well. Their summers are hot, but their winters are cold. Bison, badgers, bald eagles, coyotes, gopher snakes, antelope, jackrabbits, and mule deer live in the cold deserts.

Plants have adapted to life in the desert, too. Cacti, sagebrush, Joshua trees, and juniper trees can grow with very little water. In the cold desert, you can find sego lilies, bitterbrush, grasses, and rabbitbrush.

Wetlands

You may not think that wetlands and Utah go together. But there are close to 600,000 acres of wetlands in Utah. Wetlands are found along the banks of rivers, lakes, ponds, and streams. These are areas where water collects and keeps the soil wet.

Utah's largest wetlands are around the Great Salt Lake. We also have wetlands in the high Uintas and around Lake Powell.

The jackrabbit is a long-haired hare that lives in flat, open dry areas.

_____

Mule deer eat grass, leaves, twigs, and bark.

_____

Bulrushes grow on the banks of ponds and small rivers.

_____

Pinyon Pine are trees with yellow flowers and live in hot, dry areas.

_____

Prickly pear grows in well-drained soil that is dry and rocky.

_____

Muskrats are strong swimmers that live near freshwater and like bulrushes and cattails.

_____

Cattails are long, slender plants that live in marshy places.

_____

Beaver are small mammals that live in areas with many trees so they have enough wood to build their homes.

_____

Cougars, also known as mountain lions, live in areas with dense plant life so they can remain hidden while hunting. They typically prey on deer, elk, moose, mountain goats, wild sheep, and deer.

_____

The moose lives in wooded areas where there is snow cover in the winter and nearby lakes, bogs, swamps, streams and ponds.

_____

The coyote's diet varies depending on the seasons. It eats cactus fruit, mesquite beans, flowers, insects, rodents, lizards, rabbits, birds, and snakes.

_____

Pinyon Jay are blue birds that can be found in pinyon-juniper woodland, sagebrush, scrub oak, and sometimes in pine forests. They eat pine seeds.

_____

Red foxes like open areas in woodlands, neighborhoods, wetlands and brushy fields. They can live in more than one environment because they are so good at adapting.

_____

Red-tailed Hawks occupy just about every type of open habitat on the continent. In Utah, this includes desert, grasslands, fields and pastures, parks, and broken woodland.

_____

FIELD TRIP: BEAR RIVER MIGRATORY BIRD REFUGE

The Bear River Migratory Bird Refuge is located where the Bear River flows into the northern arm of the Great Salt Lake. It is a perfect field trip to experience wetlands. There is an education center with all sorts of information about the wetland environment and the animals that live there. You can even follow a walking trail through the wetland habitat. Be sure to take your camera!

Print some of the photos you took at the bird refuge and paste them below.

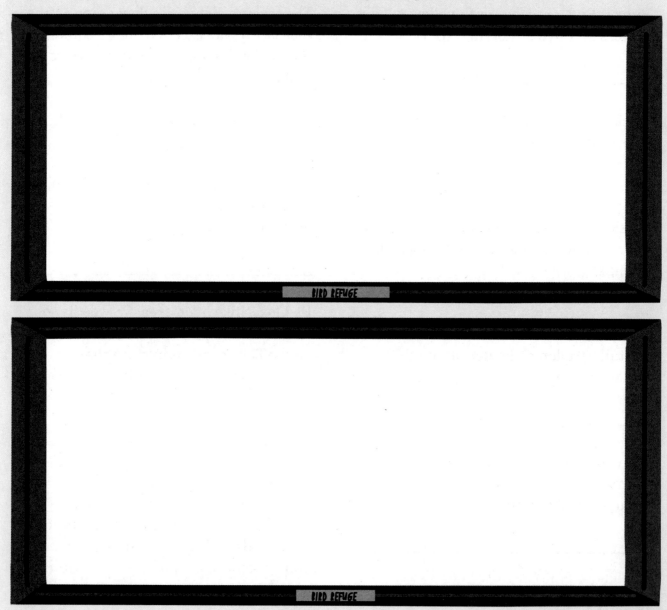

BIRD REFUGE

BIRD REFUGE

There are many visitors to the bird refuge every year and not all of them are people! Unscramble each of the clue words, using the word bank if you need a hint. Then copy the letters in the numbered cells to other cells with the same number below to find out who else visits the refuge.

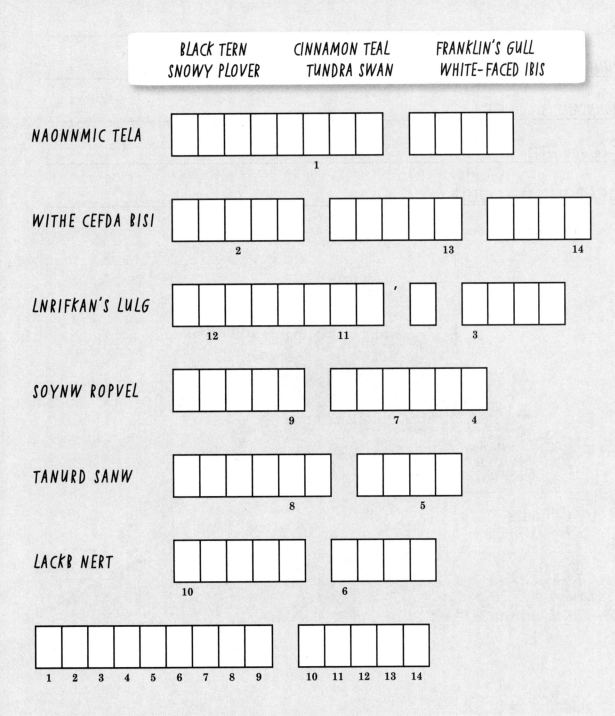

BLACK TERN   CINNAMON TEAL   FRANKLIN'S GULL
SNOWY PLOVER   TUNDRA SWAN   WHITE-FACED IBIS

NAONNMIC TELA

WITHE CEFDA BISI

LNRIFKAN'S LULG

SOYNW ROPVEL

TANURD SANW

LACKB NERT

TREES, PLEASE

More than 200 different kinds of trees grow in Utah. Utah's trees change according to elevation (how high above sea level a place is). Fill in the blanks below with the name of the tree that grows at that elevation.

HIGH PEAKS: _____

UPPER MOUNTAIN (6,000 FEET): _____

MIDDLE MOUNTAIN (5,000 FEET): _____

FOOTHILLS (4,000 FEET): _____

GRASSLANDS & DESERTS (3,000 FEET): _____

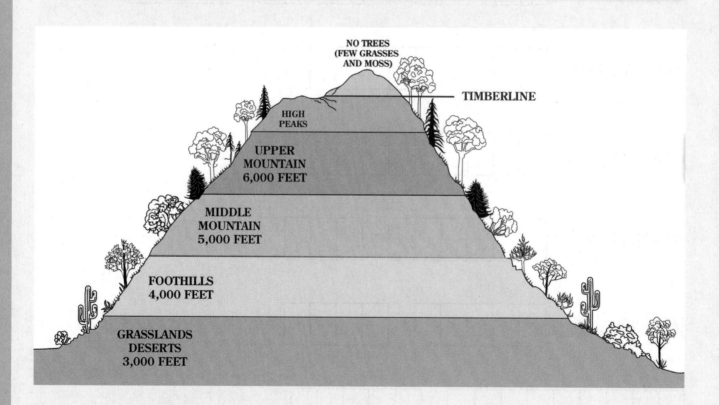

Cottonwoods are found at about 6,000 feet

Pinyon Pines are found in areas between 2,000 and 7,000 feet

Prickly Pear are usually found between 3,000 and 4,000 feet

Blue Spruce are found at about 6,000 feet

Scrub Oak are found between 5,000 and 6,000 feet

Quaking Aspen are found between 7,000 and 8,000 feet

Alpine Fir are found above 8,000 feet

Utah Juniper are usually found between 3,000 and 7,000 feet

Sage Brush are found between 6,000 and 7,000 feet

Douglas Fir are found at about 6,000 feet

UNDER PRESSURE

A fault is a fracture, or break, in the Earth's surface. Some fault lines are short and others are very long, running for miles and miles. Pressure beneath Earth's surface can cause the land to lift, fold, or dip at the faults. This is how mountains, plateaus, cliffs, and canyons were formed. Movement at these fault lines, known as earthquakes, can cause more change to the Earth's surface. Study the map showing Utah's fault lines and answer the questions.

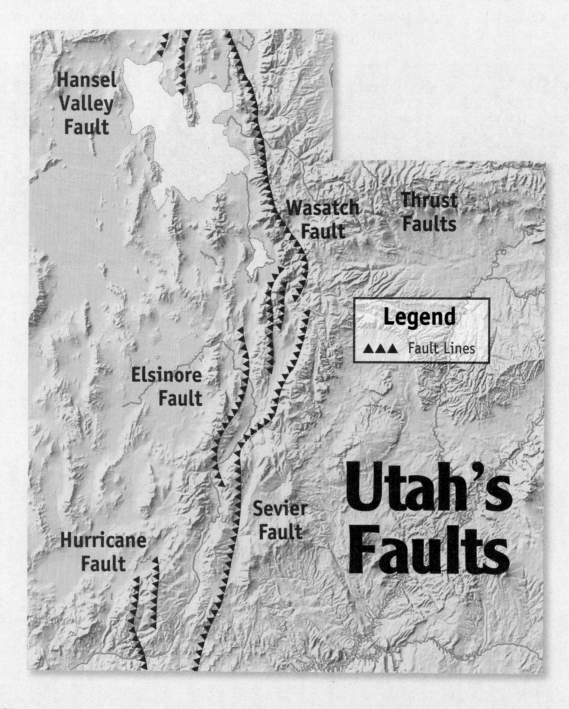

Hansel Valley Fault

Wasatch Fault

Thrust Faults

Elsinore Fault

Legend
▲▲▲ Fault Lines

Hurricane Fault

Sevier Fault

Utah's Faults

Describe the location of Utah's faults.

_____

_____

_____

_____

Where are most of Utah's faults?

_____

_____

_____

What do you notice about the landforms where there are fault lines?

_____

_____

_____

If there was an earthquake in Utah, which areas are likely to be affected?

_____

_____

_____

What message would you share with Utahns about earthquake safety?

_____

_____

_____

THE ROCK CYCLE

In Utah we live along the Rocky Mountain range. Every rock you pick up outside belongs to one of three rock groups: sedimentary, igneous, or metamorphic. Rocks belong to a rock group based on how the rock was formed. Over millions of years, rocks become each type of rock, changing as heat and pressure are applied to them.

Sedimentary: Rocks are broken down into small particles called sediment. The rocks are broken down by sun, wind, and water over long periods of time. The sediments collect in layers. Over time, these layers build up. Sometimes the minerals in the sediment dissolve in the water. They create "cement" that binds the layers together. As this happens, a solid rock is formed. Three types of sedimentary rock are found in Utah:

Igneous: Igneous rocks form when melted rock (called magma) rises from inside the earth and cools. If the magma cools beneath the surface, the cooling takes many years. The igneous rocks that form beneath the surface may have crystals in it.

If the magma cools on the surface, it cools more quickly. The rocks formed may have bubbles or be very smooth, like glass.

Sandstone (made up of tiny pieces of sand and sediment)
Conglomerate (a mix of small particles and larger pieces)
Shale (clay that has hardened due to extreme pressure)

There are four common igneous rocks in Utah:

Obsidian (a smooth, black rock that American Indians used to make spears and arrowheads)

Granite (commonly used as a building material)

Pumice (which floats because of air pockets inside of it)

Basalt (a heavy rock that contains iron; it also may contain air holes, but it will not float; many people use basalt in their yards)

Metamorphic: Metamorphic rocks have been changed inside the earth by extreme heat and pressure. These rocks may contain crystals. Sometimes the crystals are called gems because of their value. Rubies, sapphires, and garnets are found in metamorphic rocks.

Three examples of metamorphic rocks are found in Utah:

Marble (starts out as limestone, but becomes harder as heat and pressure cause the crystals to shift)

Gneiss (begins as granite, but under the heat and pressure the crystals line up and give it a banded look)

Schist (This begins as clay sediments, and erosion moves them to the bottom of a lake or shallow sea. As pressure builds, the clay becomes shale. As heat is added, it becomes slate. With more heat and pressure, it forms mica. The final step is schist.)

Draw a picture of each kind of rock in the rock cycle. Then decide which type of rock is described in the questions.

IGNEOUS

METAMORPHIC

SEDIMENTARY

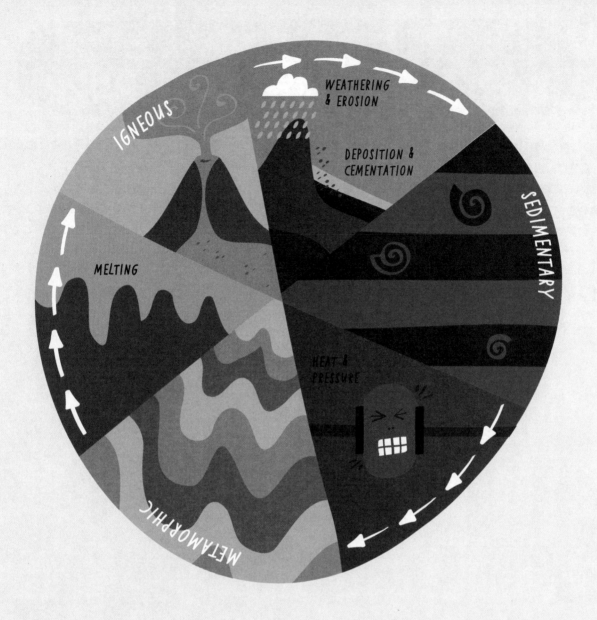

1. There was activity inside an active volcano. No magma ever made it outside of the volcano. The magma inside the volcano cooled over many years and turned into rock.

_____

2. A rocky mountain peak is beat with wind and rain over many years. The rock is broken down and the sediment gathers below the peak where it is "cemented" together.

_____

3. At a fault line, sedimentary rock is pushed beneath the earth's surface. Over many years heat and pressure are applied to the rock.

_____

FIELD TRIP: GOBLIN VALLEY STATE PARK

Goblin Valley State Park near Hanksville is a super fun place to go camping. Ask an adult to help you plan a camping trip to this unique place. It is a small state park that has thousands of sandstone hoodoo rocks (or pinnacle rocks) called goblins. Do a bit of research before you go camping to find out how these rocks were formed.

Make a drawing of the goblins you saw during your trip.

ROCK HUNT

With permission from an adult, go exploring for rocks around your home and collect six of them. Studying the rocks is a great way to learn what kind of work Mother Nature has been doing in your area over the past many, many years! Record your findings below.

Draw a picture of the rock.	Does the rock have layers or many small pieces cemented together?	Is the rock shiny or dull?	Does the rock have crystals?	Is the rock made of heavy or light material?
1.				
2.				
3.				
4.				
5.				
6.				

Choose three rocks. Use the details of the rock to draw a conclusion about which group of rocks it may belong to, igneous, sedimentary, or metamorphic.

Rock _____ is probably a _____ rock because _____.

Rock _____ is probably a _____ rock because _____

Rock _____ is probably a _____ rock because _____

EDIBLE IGNEOUS ROCKS

Have an adult help you make your own igneous rocks.

WHAT YOU WILL NEED:

1 bag white chocolate chips
1 bag milk or semisweet chocolate chips
Waxed paper
A cookie sheet
A stirring spoon
A saucepan with a double boiler

INSTRUCTIONS:

1. Fill the saucepan with water and place it on the stove. Turn on the burner and place the double boiler on top of the saucepan.

2. Place the different rock types (white and chocolate chips) in the double boiler.

3. Stir the rocks until the heat begins to combine the different rock types into hot magma.

4. Line the cookie sheet with wax paper.

5. Pour the hot magma onto the wax paper to cool, just like magma cools on the earth's surface.

6. When the chocolate magma has finished cooling, break it into pieces and enjoy your new, tasty igneous rocks!

EDIBLE SEDIMENTARY ROCKS

Have an adult help you make your own sedimentary rocks.

WHAT YOU WILL NEED:

Graham crackers
Frosting
Utensils to spread frosting

INSTRUCTIONS:

1. On a plate, place the first layer of rock sediment, a graham cracker.

2. Put some frosting on the cracker to represent the minerals that have dissolved and created cement.

3. Place another layer of rock sediment on next, a graham cracker.

4. Continue layering rocks and "cement," as many as you would like.

5. Enjoy your tasty sedimentary rock!

EDIBLE METAMORPHIC ROCKS

Have an adult help you make your own metamorphic rocks.

WHAT YOU WILL NEED:

Sugar cookie dough (dyed in three colors)
A cookie sheet
Oven or toaster oven

INSTRUCTIONS:

1. Take a small piece of each kind of rock, the different colors of cookie dough.

2. Combine all three kinds of rocks and apply pressure by smashing them all together.

3. You can even fold the dough and apply more pressure.

4. Apply heat to the rocks by baking the cookies in the oven. Follow baking directions for the sugar cookie recipe you used.

5. Once the rocks have cooled down, break one in half to see the different layers that created the metamorphic rock.

6. Enjoy your tasty metamorphic rock!

FROM WEATHERED ROCKS TO SOILS

When rocks are weathered and when plants die, their broken-down remains create soil. The soil profile is what you would see if you could cut a slice out of the earth's surface. Study the soil profile and answer the questions.

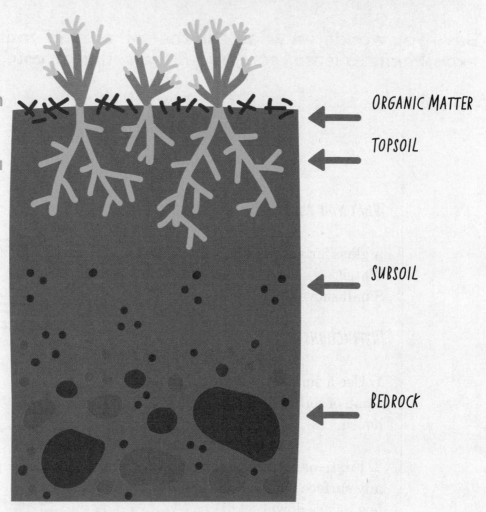

ORGANIC MATTER

TOPSOIL

SUBSOIL

BEDROCK

In which layer of the soil do plants grow?

_____

Where are the largest rocks and materials? Why do you think they are there?

_____

_____

Where are the darkest materials? Why do you think they are there?

_____

_____

WHAT'S IN YOUR SOIL?

Have you wondered what is in the soil around your house? Try this experiment to learn more about the soil near you.

WHAT YOU WILL NEED:

A glass jar with a lid
Water
Small shovel

INSTRUCTIONS:

1. Use a small shovel to get about a cup of soil from around your house.

2. First, make sure to remove any surface debris, and then dig a few inches down.

3. Put the soil in the jar.

4. Fill the jar about three-quarters full with water.

5. Put the lid on tight and shake the jar for about one minute.

6. Set down the jar and let it sit still.

7. Record your findings.

Record what you see after one minute:

_____

Record what you see after two minutes:

_____

Record what you see after five minutes:

_____

Record what you see after ten minutes:

_____

Record what you see after one day:

_____

Measure the bottom layer (sand): _____

Measure the second layer (silt): _____

Measure the top layer (clay): _____

Do you have any items still floating around in the top of the water? If so, record what you see. The floating items are organic matter, parts of dead plants and animals that become part of the soil over time.

_____

_____

_____

How would you describe your soil overall?

_____

_____

_____

Draw a picture of your soil jar. Label the different layers.

SOIL NEVER TASTED SO GOOD!

With the help of an adult, make soil profile treats for your family!

WHAT YOU WILL NEED:

Shredded coconut, slivered almonds, and gummy worms (organic matter)
Finely crushed chocolate cookies (topsoil)
Chocolate pudding (subsoil)
Candy-coated chocolate pieces (bedrock)
Clear plastic cups
Permanent marker

INSTRUCTIONS:

1. Put a layer of candy-coated chocolate pieces in the bottom of each cup.

2. Next put a layer of chocolate pudding in each cup.

3. Then put a layer crushed chocolate cookies in each cup.

4. Put a final layer of shredded coconut, slivered almonds, and gummy worms in each cup.

5. With a permanent marker, label each layer on the outside of the cups.

WORM MAZE

This poor worm is lost in the grass. Help Werner Worm find his way back to his home.

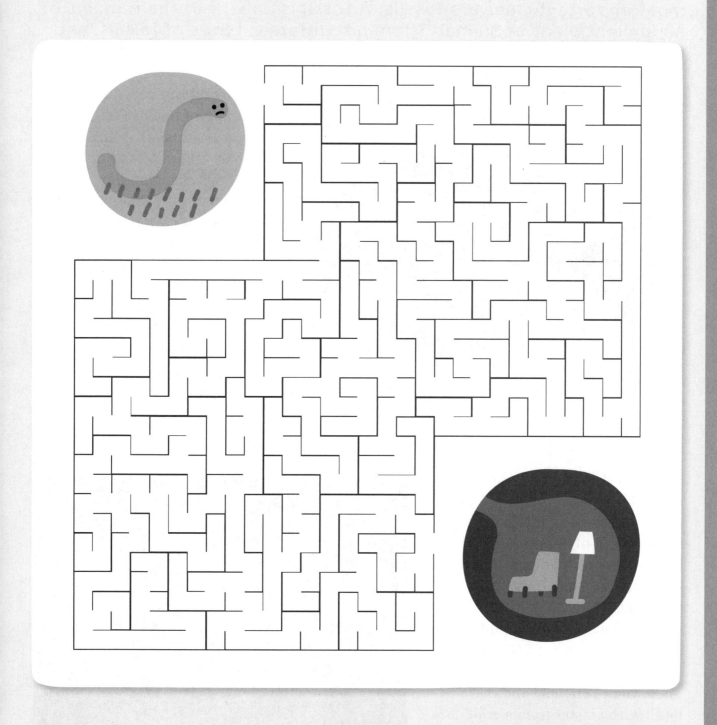

WHAT ONCE ROAMED THE EARTH

Many animals that once roamed the land in Utah are now extinct. They no longer live anywhere on Earth. How could we possibly know about creatures that lived millions of years ago? Some of the most important clues are fossils. A fossil is a mark or the remains of an ancient plant or animal. There are different types of fossils, and they are named based on how they are formed.

Impressions show the outline of a living thing. Impressions are created when thin plants and small animals die in sediment. As they rot, they leave behind a dark print of the organism. Plants, leaves, feathers, and fish often become impressions.

Make your own impression fossils with clay or dough. Using small household items, press them into clay and have others guess what the item was based on its impression.

Molds and casts are impressions made by larger organisms. When an organism dies and is covered with sediment, its body slowly breaks down. A hole, or mold, is left in its place. If the hole is filled with sediment, it produces a cast. The cast looks like the original organism on the outside.

Make your own mold and cast fossil with plaster from a craft store. Put some wet plaster in a cup. Place a small item in the

plaster, covering the top of it with the plaster. Let the plaster dry overnight. The next day, carefully chisel the plaster in half and remove the item you left in the plaster. Fill the empty mold with clay to take on the shape of the mold. Remove the clay and have others guess what the item was.

Traces are impressions that show traces of activity. These include footprints, teeth marks, tracks, and tail prints. How does a trace become a fossil? An impression must be left in soft sediment. Then the sediment hardens. It is preserved (kept the same) after being quickly covered with more sediment.

You can make your own trace fossils with leaves, paper, and crayons. Put a piece of paper over a leaf and rub the paper with the side of a peeled crayon. The crayon rubbing should reveal the shape of the leaf on the paper.

Mineral replacements form from hard body parts, such as bones, teeth, claws, or shells. These are also called petrified fossils. Over time, more and more sediment buries the remains. The bone slowly dissolves. Water filled with minerals seeps in. It replaces the bone with a rock-like material. The fossil has the same shape and size as the object but the color of the minerals. It is harder and heavier than the original.

You can make your own mineral replacement fossils with ice cube trays. If you can, use trays that make ice cubes shaped like different objects. When you fill the tray with water, it represents the water that seeps into the body part and dissolves it, leaving behind a harder and heavier material in the shape of the object.

Amber can preserve an organism whole. For example, an insect might have been trapped in tree sap. The sap slowly turns into amber, and the organism is preserved. Entire animals have also been preserved by being frozen or stuck in sticky tar pits.

You can make your own amber fossils with the help of an adult who will use a hot glue gun. On a piece of paper, have the adult cover a small item, such as a penny, with hot glue. The glue represents the amber that preserves the organism whole.

FIELD TRIP: ANCIENT UTAH

Does your family love dinosaurs? Utah is home to a number of great destinations to learn more about dinosaurs and ancient life in Utah. Keep these places in mind for your next family outing!

The Museum of Ancient Life at Thanksgiving Point in Lehi
Visit www.ThanksgivingPoint.org for more details.

The Natural History Museum of Utah in Salt Lake City
Visit www.nhmu.utah.edu for more details.

Ogden's George S. Eccles Dinosaur Park in Ogden
Visit www.dinosaurpark.org for more details.

The BYU Museum of Paleontology in Provo
Visit www.geology.byu.edu/museum for more details.

Dinosaur National Monument in Jensen
Visit nps.gov/dino for more details.

Utah Field House of Natural History in Vernal
Visit www.stateparks.utah.gov/park/utah-field-house-of-natural-history-state-park-museum for more details.

Cleveland-Lloyd Dinosaur Quarry in Price
Visit www.blm.gov/ut/st/en/fo/price/recreation/quarry.html for more details.

The Mill Canyon Dinosaur Trail in Moab
Visit www.blm.gov/ut/st/en/prog/more/cultural/Paleontology/utah_paleontology/canyon_country_paleontology/mill_canyon.html for more details.

The Dinosaur Discovery Site at Johnson Farm in St. George
Visit www.dinosite.org for more details.

The Grand Staircase-Escalante National Monument in Kanab
Visit www.blm.gov/ut/st/en/fo/grand_staircase-escalante.html for more details.

MATH

THE LARGEST GRID IN THE WORLD

You can use latitude and longitude to find a location anywhere on Earth.

LATITUDE LINES
Run side to side

Measure °North and °South of the equator

LONGITUDE LINES
Run up and down
Measure °East and °West of the prime meridian

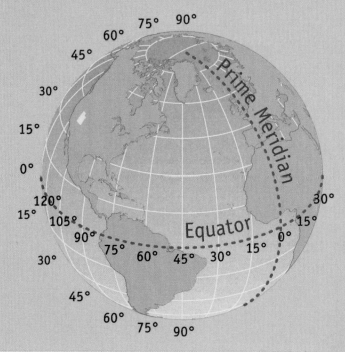

1. Utah is located between which two lines of latitude?

_____

2. Utah is located between which two lines of longitude?

_____

3. Which two continents straddle the equator?

_____

4. Which two continents straddle the prime meridian?

_____

5. Which continent is clearly located in the northern hemisphere?

6. In which hemisphere is the north pole located?

_____

7. In which hemisphere is the south pole located?

_____

8. Is Utah found in the northern or southern hemisphere?

_____

9. Is Utah found in the eastern or western hemisphere?

_____

10. How would you describe the location of Utah in both its hemispheres?

_____

UTAH'S LATITUDE AND LONGITUDE

We also use latitude and longitude lines to help us locate places in Utah. Use your grid skills to locate places within our state!

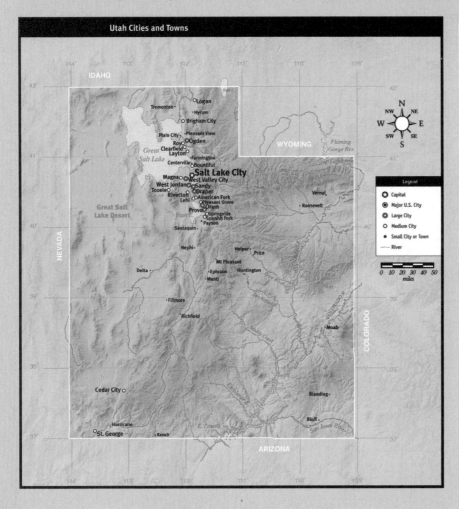

Utah Cities and Towns

1. Roosevelt, Utah is located almost exactly on which line of longitude?

_____

2. Between which two lines of latitude does it look like most people in Utah live?

_____

3. Between which two lines of longitude does it look like most people in Utah live?

_____

4. Describe the location of Vernal.

_____

5. Describe the location of Brigham City.

_____

6. Mark your city or town on the map. Describe its location.

_____

SCALE OF MILES ON A MAP

One important feature on a map is the scale of miles. A scale of miles helps us measure the distance between places. One inch on the scale might stand for 50 miles on real land. On this map, one inch is equal to 50 miles. Use a ruler to help you determine the distance between the cities below.

HOW TO USE THE SCALE OF MILES:

Measure the inches between cities x 50 miles
=
Number of miles between cities

Salt Lake City to Cedar City

_____

Salt Lake City to Moab

_____

Salt Lake City to Nephi

_____

Salt Lake City to Vernal

_____

Salt Lake City to Logan

_____

Salt Lake City to Fillmore

_____

Salt Lake City to Layton

_____

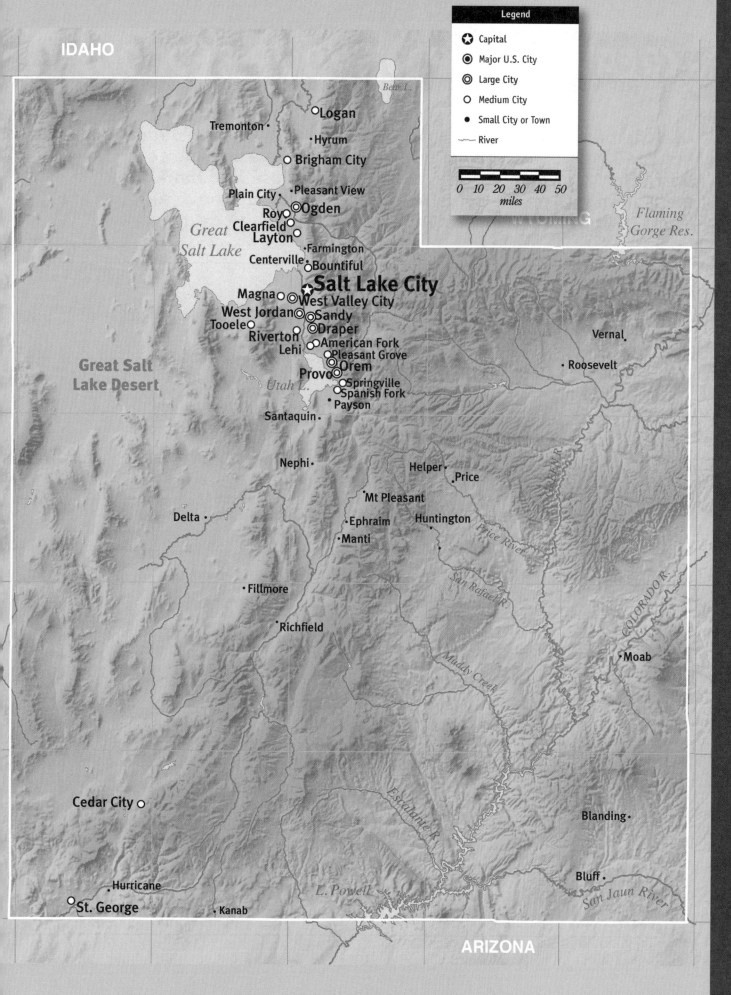

IDAHO

Legend

⭐ Capital
◉ Major U.S. City
◎ Large City
○ Medium City
• Small City or Town
～ River

0 10 20 30 40 50
miles

Bear L.

Logan
Tremonton
Hyrum
Brigham City

Plain City
Pleasant View
Ogden
Roy
Clearfield
Layton
Great
Salt Lake
Farmington
Centerville
Bountiful

Salt Lake City
Magna
West Valley City
West Jordan
Sandy
Tooele
Draper
Riverton
American Fork
Lehi
Pleasant Grove
Provo
Orem
Springville
Spanish Fork
Payson
Santaquin

Great Salt
Lake Desert
Utah L.

WYOMING

Flaming
Gorge Res.

Vernal
Roosevelt

Nephi
Helper
Price
Mt Pleasant
Delta
Ephraim
Huntington
Manti

Fillmore

Richfield

Price River
San Rafael R.
Muddy Creek
COLORADO R.
Moab

Escalante R.
Cedar City
Blanding

Bluff
Hurricane
L. Powell
St. George
Kanab
San Jaun River

ARIZONA

CREATE A MAP OF YOUR BEDROOM

Use the blank map grid below to make a map of your bedroom. Instead of a scale of miles, a scale of feet or yards will work better for your map. Decide which scale to use and mark the measurements on the scale below. Then estimate how far apart the items in your bedroom are and draw them on the grid.

<table>
<tr><td>1</td><td></td><td></td><td></td><td></td><td></td><td></td></tr>
<tr><td>2</td><td></td><td></td><td></td><td></td><td></td><td></td></tr>
<tr><td>3</td><td></td><td></td><td></td><td></td><td></td><td></td></tr>
<tr><td>4</td><td></td><td></td><td></td><td></td><td></td><td></td></tr>
<tr><td>5</td><td></td><td></td><td></td><td></td><td></td><td></td></tr>
<tr><td>6</td><td></td><td></td><td></td><td></td><td></td><td></td></tr>
<tr><td>7</td><td></td><td></td><td></td><td></td><td></td><td></td></tr>
</table>

A   B   C   D   E   F   G

SCALE

I   J   K   L   M   N   O

GOING TO GREAT LENGTHS

Did you know that Utah has over 880 miles of rivers? That's enough to stretch from Salt Lake City to Seattle, Washington! Of course none of the rivers run in a straight line. Each of Utah's ten major river systems has many branches, just like a tree. Combine the mileage of the branches for each river system to find the total length of the river and fill in the blank.

UTAH'S COLORADO RIVER SYSTEM

Total Length: _____ (Add each branch)

Cisco to Dewey Bridge	16.0
Dewey Bridge to Hittle Bottom	7.5
Goldbar to Potash Ramp	7.0
Hwy 191 Bridge to Goldbar	10.0
Moab Daily	13.0
Ruby/Horsethief Canyons	25.0
Takeout Beach to Big Bend	2.5
Westwater Canyon	17.0

UTAH'S GREEN RIVER SYSTEM

Total Length: _____ (Add each branch)

Desolation/Grey Canyons	84.0
Flaming Gorge Dam to Little Hole	7.0
Green River Daily	8.0
Indian Crossing to Colorado State Line	14.0
Labyrinth Canyon	70.0
Little Hole to Indian Crossing	9.0
Split Mountain to Sand Wash	103.5

UTAH'S DIRTY DEVIL RIVER SYSTEM

Total Length: _____ (Add each branch)

Poison Spring Crossing to State Hwy	32.0
State Hwy 24 to Poison Spring Crossing	50.0

UTAH'S MUDDY CREEK RIVER SYSTEM

Total Length: _____ (Add each branch)

Crossing to State Hwy 24	22.0
Hidden Splendor Mine to Crossing	5.0
I-70 to Lone Tree Crossing	11.0
Lone Tree X-ing to Tomdich Butte	19.0
Tomdich Butte to Hidden Splendor Mine	15.0

UTAH'S DOLORES RIVER SYSTEM

Total Length: _____ (Add each branch)

Gateway to Dewey Bridge	32.0

Utah's Price River System

Total Length: _____ (Add each branch)

Mounds Bridge to Woodside	42.0
Price Canyon	8.5
Woodside to Green River Confluence	16.0

Utah's San Juan River System

Total Length: _____ (Add each branch)

Mexican Hat to Clay Hills Crossing	58.0
Montezuma Creek to Sand Island	17.0
Sand Island to Mexican Hat	26.0

Utah's San Rafael River System

Total Length: _____ (Add each branch)

Little Grand Canyon	17.0

Utah's Virgin River System

Total Length: _____ (Add each branch)

Bloomington Gorge	12.9

Utah's White River System

Total Length: _____ (Add each branch)

Big Trujillo Wash to Bonanza Bridge	29.0
Bonanza to Mt. Fuel Bridge	40.0
Mt. Fuel Bridge to Green River	22.0
UT/CO Line to Bonanza Bridge	12.6

Organize your data!

List the river systems from shortest to longest

_____

_____

_____

_____

_____

_____

_____

_____

_____

Which river system has the greatest length?

_____

Which river system has the least length?

_____

What is the difference in length between the longest and the shortest river systems?

_____

FIELD TRIP: RIVER RAFTING

Now that you know about the major river systems in Utah, which is nearest to where you live?

_____

_____

Many people enjoy rafting trips on Utah's rivers. Maybe you and your family can plan a rafting excursion! Have an adult help you look up rafting tours and find out information for a paddling adventure on a river in Utah. It can be a river near where you live, or make it a weekend trip and go somewhere a couple hours away.

Write down information for your trip below. Include where you are going, the name of the rafting outfitter, costs, items you need to bring, how long it will take to get there, how many miles is it from your house, and if you need to make overnight plans.

_____

_____

_____

_____

_____

When you get back from your trip, write down how many miles you rafted. Did you get wet? Did you have a ton of fun?

_____

_____

_____

_____

_____

_____

Draw the expression that was on your face the first time you went over a rapid.

COMPUTE THE COMMUTE

Most people in Utah live in or around our biggest cities. Many people live in suburbs outside of the large cities and commute, or drive, to the big cities each day to work. Calculate just how far some of these commuters drive each week.

Sasha and her family live in Layton. Her dad works in Salt Lake City. Monday through Friday he drives from Layton to Salt Lake to work and back again at the end of the day. Each trip in one direction is 24 miles. How many miles does Sasha's dad commute each week?

_____

Leah is a nurse and lives in Springville. She drives to the hospital in Murray four days a week for work. Each trip in one direction is 44 miles. How many miles does Leah commute each week?

_____

Diego and his family live in Bountiful. His mom works in downtown Ogden, which is 28 miles away. She works five days a week. How many miles does Diego's mom commute each week?

_____

Does someone in your family drive to work? How far does he or she travel each day?

_____

How far does he or she travel each week?

_____

ALL THAT JAZZ

Have you ever considered a career as an NBA player? Now might be a good time to change your mind if you haven't considered it. Study the salaries of some of the NBA players on the Utah Jazz team. Answer the questions about the figures.

PLAYER	2014-15	2015-16	2016-17	2017-18	2018-19
Gordon Hayward	$14,746,000	$15,409,570	$16,073,140	$16,736,710	
Derrick Favors	$12,833,333	$11,933,333	$10983,333	$11,933,333	
Enes Kanter	$5,694,674				
Trevor Booker	$5,000,000	$4,775,000			
Dante Exum	$3,615,000	$3,777,720	$3,940,320	$4.992,385	
Steve Novak	$3,445946	$3,750,000			
Alec Burks	$3,034,356	$9,213,484	$9,904,495	$10,595,506	$11,286,515
Trey Burke	$2,548,560	$2,658,240	$3,386,598		
Jeremy Evans	$1,794,871				
Rodney Hood	$1,290,360	$1,348,440	$1,406,520	$2,386,864	
Rudy Gobert	$1,127,400	$1,175,880	$2,121,288		
Touré Murry	$1,000,000	$1,000,000			
Ian Clark	$816,482				
Joe Ingles	$507,336				
Carrick Felix	$816,482				
Dee Bost	$65,000				
Jack Cooley	$65,000				
Kevin Murphy	$65,000				
Jordan Hamilton	$25,000				

source: http://www.basketball-reference.com/contracts/UTA.html

1. Who is the highest paid player for the 2014–2015 season?

_____

2. Which players, if any, made the same amount of money during the 2014–2015 season?

_____

3. What is the difference in salary between the highest and lowest paid players in the 2104–2015 season?

_____

4. What is the difference between the highest and the second highest salary during the 2014–2015 season?

_____

5. What is the increase in salary between each of the seasons shown for Gordon Hayward?

_____

6. If Gordon Hayward still plays with the Jazz in the 2018–2019 season, what might his salary be?

_____

7. What is the increase in salary between each of the seasons shown for Alec Burks?

_____

8. What is the average, or mean, salary of a Jazz player during the 2014–2015 season? To find the average, or mean, add up all the salaries, and divide that number by the number of salaries you added.

_____

9. What is the mode of the Jazz players' salaries during the 2014–2015 season? The mode is the piece of data (salary) that appears most often in a set of data.

_____

10. What is the median, or middle, salary of Jazz players during the 2014–2015 season? To find the median, plot each salary on the number line below. Repeat salaries count as one mark on a number line. Which salary or salaries land in the middle position? If it is one salary in the middle, that is your median. If you have two salaries in the middle, find the average of the two and that is your median.

```
1   2   3   4   5   6   7   8   9   10   11   12   13   14   15   16   17
```

FIELD TRIP: JAZZ GAME

Are you a Jazz fan? Have you ever been to a game? Now that you know so much about the players' salaries, you should go to a game and see what they do to earn their pay! If you can't actually go to a game, watch one on TV.

What team did the Jazz play against in the game you watched?

_____

What was the final score?

_____

Did the players with the highest salaries play in the game more than those with lower salaries?

_____

Basketball players are really tall! Look at the roster from the game (or look it up online) and see if you can figure out who the tallest player is on the team.

_____

By looking at the heights of all the players on the roster, what is your best guess for the average height of the team?

_____

How tall are you? _____

Who is taller, you or the tallest player on the team?

_____

Taller by how much?

_____

HOW FAR IS A MILE?

The first people who lived in Utah did a lot of walking. They likely walked a mile or more each day to hunt or gather food. They walked everywhere they went! Can you imagine if you had to walk everywhere you went—to get to school, to buy groceries, to see the doctor, to visit a family member?

Have you ever walked or ran a mile? It can feel like a really long distance. A mile is 5,280 feet. How many yards are in a mile? You can convert the length from feet to yards as long as you know how many feet are in a yard.

> THERE ARE _____ FEET IN A YARD.

Now, we need to see how many groups of three feet are in the total 5,280 miles. When we talk about "groups of" we are either using multiplication or division. Since we know we are looking for an amount smaller that 5,280 we are using division.

> 5,280 FEET ÷ _____ FEET = _____ YARDS (THE NUMBER OF YARDS IN A MILE)

Now it's time to walk the walk! Walk or run a mile with a family member. Talk to them about what it would be like if you had to walk everywhere you went.

SPIRALING AROUND

The Spiral Jetty at Rozel Point on the Great Salt Lake was created by artist Robert Smithson in 1970. He used six thousand tons of black basalt rock and earth from the site to make a coil 1,500 feet long and 15 feet wide that winds counterclockwise from the shore into the water. The water level and salt from the water constantly change the look of the jetty.

Have an adult help you look up different kinds of spirals on the Internet, and then draw some examples of what you found below.

A fun family outing could be a trip to the Spiral Jetty in Box Elder County. If the lake water is low enough, you can walk the entire length of the jetty. What do you notice as you walk?

Is 1,500 feet a long walk?

_____

How wide does 15 feet seem?

_____

_____

_____

What do the rocks look like?

_____

_____

_____

_____

What do you notice about the water?

_____

_____

_____

_____

_____

The spiral shape shows up in nature all the time. Name a few places or things in nature that have a spiral.

_____

_____

_____

_____

_____

THE BEES' KNEES

The Salt Lake Bees baseball team is a AAA affiliate of the Anaheim Angels and the Pacific Coast League. Many people in Utah enjoy watching a professional baseball team play games. Find the answers to the math problems below and then use the letters to break the code to finish a fun Bees' fact.

Add or subtract. Regroup if needed.

I 4,121 + 4,093	T 5,902 + 8,850	A 9,328 + 7,477	B 2,857 + 8,149	E 7,529 + 9,342
P 8,939 - 826	D 4,824 - 3,912	K 5,670 - 3,333	C 10,296 - 3,053	M 8,642 - 2,468
L 3,573 + 5,441	R 4,805 - 2,604	N 1,999 + 6,529	H 7,461 - 5,509	Y 429 - 421

THE BEES PLAY THEIR GAMES _____ _____   _____
                          8,214 8,528   16,805

_____ _____ _____ _____ _____ _____ _____ _____
11,006 16,805 9,014 9,014 8,113 16,805 2,201 2,337

_____ _____ _____ _____ _____ _____ _____ _____ _____
8,528 8,214 7,243 2,337 8,528 16,805 6,174 16,871 912

_____ _____ _____   _____ _____ _____ _____ _____ _____ *
14,752 1,952 16,871   16,805 8,113 8,214 16,805 2,201 8

*Look up this word in a dictionary to see what it means and how it applies to the Bees.

FIELD TRIP: BUZZIN' FOR BASEBALL

Take me out to the ball game! It is always fun to attend a Bees' game and watch some buzzing baseball action. If you and your family or friends get a chance, head to Smith's Ballpark in Salt Lake City and take in a game. Maybe you will get to meet the team mascot—Bumble!

Fill in the scoreboard for the game you watched.

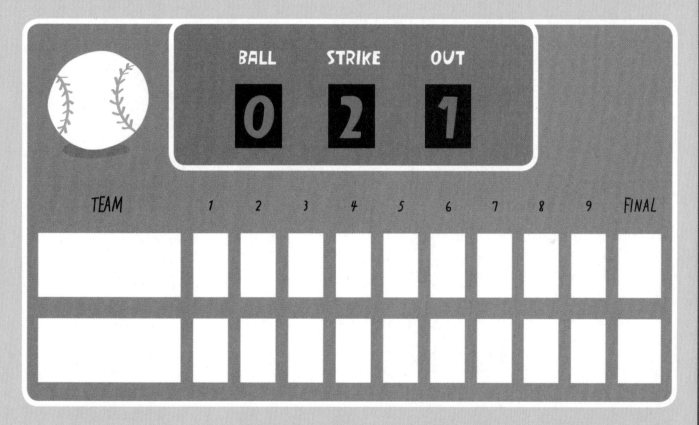

SMITH'S BALLPARK

GRIZZLY GOALS

The Utah Grizzlies professional hockey team just played a roaring game against the Colorado Eagles. The final score was grrrreat! Solve the below math problems and then add up the answers to see who won the game.

Place the answers from group A on the Grizzlies' pucks and the answers from group B on the Eagles' pucks. Then add each column. The team with the highest total won the game.

A		GRIZZLIES	B		EAGLES
8 x 8	=		5 x 3	=	
40 ÷ 5	=		20 ÷ 4	=	
6 x 7	=		6 x 8	=	
81 ÷ 9	=		7 ÷ 7	=	
3 x 7	=		9 x 3	=	
16 ÷ 4	=		100 ÷ 2	=	

Total _____   Total _____

Who won the game? _____

FIELD TRIP: HOCKEY FUN

The Utah Grizzlies Hockey Team plays their home games at the Maverick Center in West Valley City.

Do some online research with an adult and find out when you could attend a game and how to get tickets. Write down the information below.

_____

_____

_____

_____

_____

Hockey is a very fast-paced game and players often get carried away and break the rules. When this happens, the players and their team are given penalties. Keep track of the penalties each team receives at the game you attend. Which team got the most?

HOME	AWAY
PENALTIES	PENALTIES

STATE SYMBOLS

Utah has its own state symbols. Each symbol shows something special about our state. School children from Utah helped choose some of our state symbols.

State Animal
Rocky Mountain Elk

State Bird
California Gull

State Fish
Bonneville Cutthroat Trout

State Insect
Honey Bee

State Tree
Blue Spruce

State Flower
Sego Lily

State Fruit
Cherry

State Rock
Coal

State Gem
Topaz

State Mineral
Copper

State Fossil
Allosaurus

State Song
"Utah, This Is The Place"

GLOSSARY

A

adapt: to change in order to survive; to adjust to new conditions

adobe: a kind of clay that can be made into bricks

agriculture: the science or practice of farming

allegiance: loyalty

amendment: a change or addition to the Constitution

ancestor: a relative who came before you

appoint: to assign a job or role to someone

archaeology: the study of history through artifacts, bones, and ruins

artifact: an object people made or used and then left behind

atomic: relating to atoms or nuclear energy

B

barter: to trade or exchange goods or services without the use of money

basin: a large, low, flat area surrounded by mountains or high plateaus

bill: an idea for a law

biofuel: fuel made from living matter

boom: a period of fast growth

boycott: to refuse to buy something in order to make a point

C

cache: a collection of items stored or hidden, or a hiding place for such items

canal: a man-made waterway that connects to other waterways

census: the official count of a population

century: a period of 100 years

ceremony: a ritual or special act

charity: help or money that people give to others

citizen: a person who lives legally in a city, town, or country

civic organization: a group of citizens who get together to work toward a common purpose

civil rights: the basic rights of every citizen of our country

civilize: to bring to a higher stage of education and culture

clan: a group of related families

climate: the general pattern of weather, year after year colony: a settlement under the control of another country

communication: contact with the outside world; the act of sending information back and forth

commute: to travel some distance between home and work

compass rose: a symbol on a map that shows direction (North, South, East, West)

compromise: to reach an agreement by having each side give up something it wants

concentration camp: a prison camp for Jews and others in Europe during World War II

condense: to get thicker or more dense

conflict: a serious disagreement or argument

conquer: to take over by military force

conserve: to save or protect for the future

constitution: a written plan of government

consumer: a person who buys or uses goods and services

continent: one of the seven large land areas of the world

convert: a person who has changed his religious faith

county: a political region within a state

culture: the way of life of a particular group of people

custom: a traditional or usual way of doing something

D

defend: to resist an attack made on someone or something

demand: the desire of consumers for a particular good or service

democracy: a form of government in which the people rule

depression: a time when many people are out of work and cannot make enough money to care for their families

descendant: a person who comes from a particular ancestor

desegregate: to end segregation or separation by race

desert: a place that gets very little rain

develop: to grow and become more advanced or mature

discrimination: treating someone unfairly because of the color of their skin, whether they are male or female, or whether they are rich or poor

district: a part of a larger place

diverse: showing a lot of variety or differences

E

earthquake: a sudden shaking of the ground as a result of movement in the Earth's crust.

economics: the study of how people get the goods and services they need and want

economy: a way of making a living; how people produce, sell, and buy goods and services

elect: to choose by voting

elevation: how high the land is above sea level

empire: a group of territories under the control of one country or ruler

endanger: to bring into danger

enforce: to make someone obey a rule or law

entrepreneur: a person who starts a business

environment: the setting in which something lives

equality: the state of being equal

erosion: the wearing away of land by wind and water

ethnic: referring to a group with a common culture, usually a subgroup

evaporate: to turn from liquid into vapor or steam

excavate: to remove earth in order to find something buried

expedition: a journey made by a group of people for a particular purpose

explorer: a person who travels to a new place in order to learn about or sometimes claim land

export: to send out to another country for sale

F

fault: a crack in the Earth's surface

federal: relating to the central or national government of the United States

fertile: able to produce crops

fossil: a mark or the remains of an ancient plant or animal

fossil fuel: a natural fuel such as coal or gas that was formed over time from the remains of plants and animals

found: to establish

freight: goods transported by ship, train, truck, or aircraft

fur trade: a business where animal fur is traded for other things or for money

G

generator: a machine that produces electricity

geography: the study of the land, its people and places, and its environments

glacier: a huge mass of ice

globalization: the act or process of making things involve the entire world; free trade around the world

goods: products that are made, bought, and sold

gorge: a narrow valley with steep walls and streams running through it

government: the governing body of a nation, state, or community

grid: a network of lines that cross each other to form squares or rectangles

guarantee: to promise

H

harmony: agreement, working well together

hemisphere: half of the Earth

heritage: all the traditions that are passed down through generations

Hispanic: a Latin American who speaks Spanish

historic: having to do with written history

history: the story of the past

hogan: an American Indian home made from logs and earth

Holocaust: the killing of European Jews and others in Nazi concentration camps during World War II

hunter-gatherer: someone who moves around to hunt and gather food

hydroelectricity: electricity that is produced by moving water

I

immigrant: a person who moves to a new country to live

impact: the effect of one thing upon another

import: to bring something into a country in order to sell it

income: money received for work

industry: a type of business or activity that makes money

inference: a conclusion you reach by studying the facts and thinking

influence: to have an effect on someone or something

interact: to act upon one another; to act in such a way as to affect another

internment camp: a camp where people are kept for political or military reasons

inversion: when a layer of warm air traps cold air and leads to a build-up of air pollution

irrigate: to bring water to crops

isolated: alone or apart from others

J

justice: fairness; fair behavior or treatment

L

labor union: a group of workers who get together to protect their rights and make their jobs better

landform: a natural feature of the land

Latino: a person who comes to the United States from Latin America

latitude: a line running east-west, used to describe location on the Earth

legend: a key that shows what the symbols on a map represent; a story that explains how something came to be

legislature: a group of people who make the laws

liberty: freedom; the state of being free

longitude: a line running north-south, used to describe location on the Earth

loyal: showing constant support or allegiance

M

manufacture: to make things in factories or with machines

mass transit: a way for a lot of people to get around; public transportation

migrant: tending to move from place to place

migrate: to move from one area to settle in another

mission: a small religious community where priests and others lived; a group of people taking part in a religious assignment

missionary: a person sent on a religious mission; a person who travels to other places to teach people a religion

moderate: avoiding extremes; tending to the middle; not too cold and not too hot

N

native: born in a place or being naturally from a place

natural resource: something found in nature that people can use

O

ore: solid material from which metal or minerals can be separated

organism: a tiny living thing

P

passenger: a traveler on board

permanent: lasting

persecute: to treat someone badly because of religious beliefs or race

petition: an official written request

physical: having to do with the natural land and landforms

pioneer: a person who is among the first to move to a new place

plains: a large area of flat land with few trees

plateau: a high, wide, flat area of land

point of view: a particular way of seeing something

political party: a group of people who share the same ideas about government

polluted: made dirty or toxic with harmful elements

population: all the people who live in a place

poverty: the state of being very poor

precipitation: the amount of water in the air that falls as rain, hail, sleet, or snow

prehistoric: before written history

prejudice: a negative judgement made about another person, often based on a person's race or religion

preserve: to maintain or keep alive

prevention: the act of stopping something from happening

primary source: something created by someone who was there an the time, a firsthand account

privilege: a right, advantage, or opportunity

producer: a person who produces or sells goods or services

profit: the money left after expenses are paid

progress: forward or onward movement

prohibit: to forbid or not allow something

R

rare: not happening very often

ration: a fixed amount of something that is allowed to each person during a time of shortage or war

rebel: to resist authority or control, to rise up against a government or ruler

recreation: things people do for fun when they are not working

refinery: a place where oil is refined, or made pure by removing the parts not needed

refugee: a person who is forced to leave his or her country to escape war or natural disaster

region: an area that has things in common, a land division based on common features

religion: a set of beliefs about God and the universe

rendezvous: a large gathering of fur traders where furs and supplies were bought, sold, and traded

representative: a person elected to speak or act for a group of people

representative democracy: a type of government in which the people choose representatives to vote and make the laws for them

reservation: land set aside for American Indians

reservoir: a large lake made by people to collect and store water

resist: to withstand the action or effect of something

resort: a place where people stay while on vacation or go for a day of fun

respect: a high regard for something or someone

responsibility: a duty, something you are in charge of doing

right: a privilege citizens are entitled to

ruin: the remains of an old building

rule of law: the idea that no one is above the law; the law is the highest power

rural: having to do with the countryside rather than a town or city

S

scarce: in short supply; hard to get enough of

secondary source: something created by someone who was not there at the time, a second-hand account

sediment: matter that settles to the bottom of a liquid or body of water

segregate: to separate by race

seismic: relating to earthquakes or other vibrations of the Earth and its crust

self-sufficient: needing no outside help in satisfying one's needs

services: work done for another person for money

severe: very great or intense

slave: a person owned by another who is forced to work without pay

smelter: a place where minerals are taken out of the rock and turned into metal

sovereignty: self rule; supreme power or authority

statehood: the status of being recognized as state instead of just a territory

stock: a small share of a company that can be bought or sold

suburb: areas located outside a city

suffrage: the right to vote

supply: how much of something there is

surrender: to give in to an opponent

survivor: one who survives or stays alive after an event in which others have died

T

tax: money people must pay to the government to pay for services

technology: the use of scientific knowledge for industry and other purposes

telegraph: a system for sending messages from a distance along a wire

temperature: the degree of heat present in something

territory: a land region owned and ruled by a country, a region that is not a state

textile: cloth that is woven or knit by machines

theocracy: a form of government in which priests or religious leaders rule in the name of God

tipi: an American Indian home made of tall wooden poles and buffalo skins

tornado: a mass of swirling winds that moves across the ground during a storm

tourism: the industry of making money from people who visit

trading post: a store or small settlement established for trading

traditional: according to tradition or the ways of the past

transcontinental: going across a continent

translator: a person who changes one language into another

transportation: the act of moving people or goods from one place to another

treaty: a written agreement between two groups

tribe: a group of people from the same family or culture

trust land: land that the U.S. government gave to Utah as a way to make money for education

U

unemployment: the state of being without a job

urban: having to do with a city

V

veto: to say no to a bill; to prevent from becoming a law

violence: the use of force to hurt or kill someone

volunteer: someone who helps out without getting paid; to offer to do something

W

wagon train: a line of wagons traveling together

welfare: money or support given to the poor by an organization

wetlands: land consisting of marshes or swamps

wickiup: an American Indian home made from branches and grasses

wildfire: a forest or brush fire that spreads quickly

ANSWER KEY

VOCABULARY

Geography and Population (page 20)

1. D
2. B
3. E
4. F
5. A
6. C

Geography and Our Safety (page 23)

1. rare
2. tornado
3. wildfire
4. inversion
5. prevention
6. polluted
7. severe

The Story of the Past (page 28)

1. history
2. archaeology
3. ruin
4. culture
5. artifact
6. secondary source
7. excavate
8. primary source

Learning About the Past Word Search (page 29)

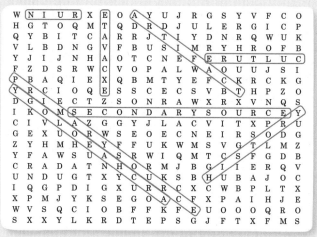

About the Past Crossword Puzzle (page 35)

Across

5. heritage
7. legend

Down

1. descendant
2. traditional
3. preserve
4. respect
6. harmony

The Fur Trade Maze (page 39)

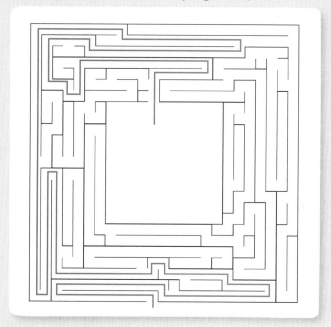

Life in the Utah Territory (page 46)

1. C
2. B
3. A
4. F
5. E
6. D

Changes for American Indians (page 47)

1. disagreement, argument
2. attack
3. resist, rise, government
4. land, Indians
5. effect
6. give, opponent
7. written agreement

New Groups of Immigrants (page 53)

Across

3. ethnic
4. labor union
5. segregate

Down

1. discrimination
2. influence

Changes in 20th Century Word Scramble (page 63)

amendment
boycott
civil rights
desegregate
diverse
justice
progress
Special word: equality

GEOGRAPHY & SOCIAL STUDIES

Map Terms Word Search (page 81)

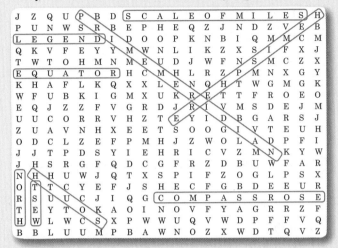

A Map by Any Other Name . . . Would Still Be a Map (page 82)

It tells us how many inches of rain each shade of blue represents; the darker the shade, the more rain an area has.

The title should include something about Utah and the amounts of rain/precipitation.

Population Map of Utah (page 84)

1. Green
2. Gray
3. Utah's cities with the highest populations are near the Great Salt Lake, along the Wasatch Front, or in the southern half of Utah.
4. Any cities represented in gray on the map.
5. Any cities represented in the green on the map.
7. Answers may include challenges related to living in the desert or living away from other cities where people and stores can be found.

Land Features Crossword Puzzle (page 87)

Across

2. streams
6. rivers
7. mountains

Down

1. valleys
3. plateaus
4. basins
5. lakes
6. mountain range

Do You Know the National Parks? (page 92)

1. Arches
2. Canyonlands
3. Zion
4. Capitol Reef
5. Bryce Canyon

Utah's State & National Parks (page 95)

1. Some might say national government and some might say state; answer should be supported by evidence from the map.
2. The national forests are found in the same location as Utah's mountain ranges.
3. Two
4. Seven
5. It is located west of the southern tip of the Great Salt Lake.

Find the Hidden Term (page 98)

Rocky Mountain Elk
California Gull
Bonneville Cutthroat Trout
Honey Bee
Blue Spruce
Sego Lily
Cherry
Coal
Topaz
Copper
Allosaurus
"Utah, This is the Place"
Hidden term: State Symbols

Indian Tribal Lands (page 108)

Ute
Navajo
Goshute
Ute
Shoshone and Ute mostly
Shoshone and Ute mostly

Find the Indian Peoples Word Search (page 111)

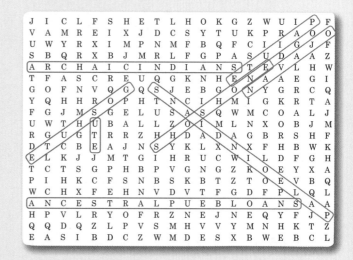

Which Way Did He Go? (page 112)

1. He turns and heads west.
2. He likely began following the same trail as the Dominguez-Escalante expedition.
3. Probably the western half of the state; it is dry and hot there with fewer bodies of water.
4. The region spanning from the northeast corner to the southwest corner; it may have something to do with following the mountain range and bodies of water.
5. His route goes through the area that would later be named after him, Lake Powell.

Trick question: The country of the United States wasn't created until 1776. Before then, the states were just British colonies.

Trapper Routes (page 114)

1. William H. Ashley, Peter Skene Ogden, Joseph Walker, and Antoine Robidoux
2. mountains
3. There are fewer mountains, and it is dry and hot there. That means fewer animals are able to live there.
4. Etienne Provost
5. Peter Skene Ogden and Etienne Provost

Fact or Fiction? (page 115)

True
False; their wives and families often traveled with them.
True
True
False; most died of old age.
False; trapping was a business and mountain men made money from it.
False; while some were brave, creative, and hardworking, some were also greedy, violent, and racist.
True
True

Migration Maze (page 117)

READING & WRITING

Cite Text Evidence: Ancient Lake Bonneville (page 124)

Paragraph 2—Long ago, Utah's climate began to get warmer, melting snow and ice. Paragraph 3—The water ran down the canyons into a growing lake.

The lake was huge and spread over the Great Basin. It spread through canyons and valleys. It covered much of western Utah. It was over 1,000 feet deep. Paragraph 3

It overflowed into Idaho and into the Snake and Columbia Rivers. Paragraph 4

The lake formed a bench that you can see along the mountains today. Paragraph 5
At areas where mountain streams entered the lake, there is rich soil that was carried down from the mountains. Paragraph 6

They are smaller lakes that remain from the dried up Lake Bonneville.

The last sentence: The Great Salt Lake, Utah Lake, and Sevier Lake are all that is left of the ancient lake today.

National Parks (page 142)

Lines 2 and 3; Park rangers hired by the government.

Line 4; Zion National Park

Lines 6 and 7 (possibly 8); Ancestral Puebloan Indians, Southern Paiutes, and possibly some Mormons.

Lines 9, 10, and 11; Deep gorges, huge rock towers, and three major rivers.

Lines 11, 12, and 13; Freemont Indians once hunted in Canyonlands. Later the Ancestral Puebloans farmed there.

Lines 11 and 12; They may be from the Fremont Indians or Ancestral Puebloans who once lived there.

Lines 15 and 16; Rock art shows that American Indians lived there for many years.

Line 18; It got its name from its stone arches.

Lines 23 and 24; Bryce Canyon is one of the most colorful parks in the world with white, yellow, red, orange, and purple rocks.

Lines 24 and 25; Wind, ice, and water carve the rocks into many shapes.

Five Historic Tribes Brain Teaser (page 158)

1. tipis
2. Goshute
3. Hogan
4. Ute
5. Paiute
6. Navajo
7. Shoshone
8. horses
9. cradleboards
10. arrows

Legends (page 162)

Coyote and a large bird

Mountain Man Scramble (page 169)

Etienne Provost
Jim Bridger
Peter Skene Ogden
Louis Vasquez
James Beckwourth
Jedediah Smith
Answer: Showing off their skills at rendezvous

SCIENCE

It's Natural! (page 188)

1. Answers will vary.
2. Answers may include copper, gold, silver, lead, salt, clay, sand, and gravel.
3. Because all of those counties surround the Great Salt Lake
4. Coal, uranium, oil/petroleum, natural gas, and timber
5. Limestone, sand and gravel
6. Uranium is found in the southern half of the state.
7. The Great Salt Lake Desert covers much of the western part of the state. Trees don't grow in deserts.
8. Salt, copper, uranium, oil/petroleum, natural gas, clay, timber, limestone, and sand and gravel are likely to be found in southern Colorado because they are found in the southern part of Utah that borders Colorado.
9. Salt, copper, uranium, limestone, oil/petroleum, clay, timber, natural gas, and sand and gravel
10. Dagget and Rich Counties

Utah's Natural Resources Word Search (page 191)

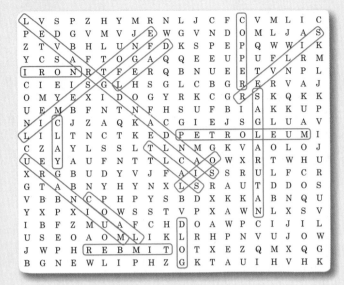

The Lake Effect (page 196)

1. Cold air moves over warm lake waters.
2. The warmed air rises, taking moisture with it.
3. Clouds form.
4. Rain and snow fall over the lake and on the shore.

Utah's Three Climates (page 198)

Steppe

Desert

Highland (Mountain)

A Climo-what? (page 200)

1. red
2. blue
3. ten degrees
4. with blue bars
5. June and July
6. December and January
7. high in the winter and low in the summer
8. high in the winter and low in the summer
9. more precipitation in the winter, spring, and fall.

Wonderful Water (page 202)

1. Evaporation
2. Condensation
3. Precipitation
4. Collection

Three Regions, Three Environments (page 206)

desert

forest

wetlands

desert

desert

wetlands

wetlands

forest or wetlands

forest

forest

desert

forest

forest and wetlands

desert, wetlands, and some forest areas

Wild Bird Scramble (page 209)

Cinnamon teal

White-faced ibis

Franklin's gull

Snowy plover

Tundra swan

Black tern

Answer: migratory birds

Under Pressure (page 212)

The Wasatch, Elsinore, Sevier, and Hurricane Faults run north and south through the middle of Utah. The Thrust Fault is in the northeast corner of Utah. The Hansel Valley Fault is in the northwest corner of Utah.

Most of Utah's faults run north and south through the center of the state.

There are mountains where each of the fault lines are found.

The areas that are in and around the mountains; the center of the state, from the north to the south; the northeast corner of the state; the northwest corner of the state.

People who live along or near the fault lines should be prepared to handle and earthquake.

The Rock Cycle (page 214)

1. igneous
2. sedimentary
3. metamorphic

From Weathered Rocks to Soils (page 223)

Plants are the organic matter, and they grow in the topsoil.

The larger materials are at the bottom of the soil profile. They are heavier, so they sink to the bottom and the lighter materials stay on top.

The topsoil and organic matter are darkest. The topsoil contains the most dead material, nutrients, and water.

Worm Maze (page 227)

MATH

Largest Grid in the World (page 234)

1. Between 30 degrees north and 45 degrees north
2. Between 105 degrees west and 120 degrees west
3. South America and Africa
4. Europe and Africa
5. North America
6. The northern hemisphere
7. The southern hemisphere
8. Northern
9. Western
10. Utah is located in the northwestern hemisphere

Utah's Latitude and Longitude (page 235)

1. 110 degrees west
2. Between 40 degrees north and 41 degrees north
3. Between 112 degrees west and 111 degrees west
4. Vernal is about halfway between 40 and 41 degrees north and about halfway between 109 and 110 degrees west.
5. Brigham City is almost 112 degrees west and about halfway between 41 and 42 degrees north.
6. Answers will vary.

Scale of Miles on a Map (page 236)

About 210 miles

About 190 miles

About 125 miles

About 120 miles

About 65 miles

About 70 miles

About 22 miles

Going to Great Lengths (page 240)

98

82

32

295.5

72

66.5

101

17

12.9

103.6

Virgin, San Rafael, Dolores, Price, Muddy Creek, Dirty Devil, Colorado, San Juan, White, Green

Green River System

Virgin River System

282.6 miles

Compute the Commute (page 243)

240 miles

352 miles

280 miles

All That Jazz (page 244)

1. Gordon Hayward
2. Dee Bost, Jack Cooley, and Kevin Murphy
3. $14,721,000
4. $1,912,667
5. From 2014–2015 to 2015–2016 the increase is $663,570.

    From 2015–2016 to 2016–2017 the increase is $663,570.

    From 2016–2017 to 2017–2018 the increase is $663,570.
6. Increase his salary by the same amount as the three previous seasons; $17,400,280.
7. From 2014–2015 to 2015–2016 the increase is $6,179,128.

    From 2015–2016 to 2016–2017 the increase is $691,011.

    From 2016–2017 to 2017–2018 the increase is $691,011.

    From 2017–2018 to 2018–2019 the increase is $691,009.

8. $2,927,790
9. Jeremy Evans' salary is the median, $1,794,871.
10. $65,000

How Far Is a Mile? (page 247)

3

3 feet, 1760 yards

The Bees' Knees (page 250)

I. 8,214

T. 14,752

A. 16,805

B. 11,006

E. 16,871

P. 8,113

D. 912

K. 2,337

C. 7,243

M. 6,174

L. 9,014

R. 2,201

N. 8,528

H. 1,952

Y. 8

The Bees play their games in a ballpark nicknamed the Apiary.

Grizzly Goals (page 252)

A. 64; 8; 42; 9; 21; 4

B. 15; 5; 48; 1; 27; 50

Grizzlies' total: 148

Eagles' total: 146

Grizzlies win